Bathrooms

Kevin McCloud left Cambridge with a degree in History of Art and Architecture before training and working as a theatre designer and scenic artist. He has become well known for his interior design work and has written many books, including the bestseller, *Kevin McCloud's Decorating Book* and his latest, *The Complete Decorator*. As well as regular appearances on radio and BBC *Home Front*, he also presents BBC2's *Home Front in the Garden*, writes newspaper and magazine columns and is a director of McCloud & Co. Ltd., a lighting and manufacturing company specialising in highly crafted and decorative items.

He lives and farms in Somerset.

Bathrooms

KEVIN MCCLOUD

BBC Books

For Milo

Principal photography: Paul Bricknell
Illustrations: Claire Davies

Other photography: John Heseltine and George Taylor

This book is published to accompany the
BBC Television series *Home Front*.

Series Producer: Mary Sackville-West
Editor: Daisy Goodwin

Published by BBC Books, an imprint of
BBC Worldwide Ltd.,
Woodlands, 80 Wood Lane, London W12 0TT

First published 1998

ISBN 0 563 38390 9

Edited and designed for BBC Books
by Phoebus Editions Ltd

Set in Futura
Printed and bound in France by Imprimerie Pollina s.a.
Colour separations by Imprimerie Pollina s.a.
Cover printed by Imprimerie Pollina s.a.

Contents

Foreword

When, as the *Home Front* team, we were
planning this series of books and debating
who should write which, I leapt at the
opportunity of this one. Bathrooms, more than
kitchens, or even dining rooms (the showiest
of places) are, I think, the room in a house
where our fantasies can be given free rein. It
is a place of hedonistic pursuit, of pure

enjoyment and relaxation, of pampering and even contemplation.

Yet it is often also, of course, the one fully plumbed room in the house
and so most of us have to shoehorn bath and basin in with the toilet
and, perhaps, the bidet. It has always struck me how odd this is. I
suppose it is part of the British practical mentality: putting basic bodily
functions in the same room as recreational activities like bathing
represents an economy of building practice. But, (and let me here use
this foreword to make a plea), if you have the opportunity, put the two
functions in different rooms. Users of both facilities will thank you for it
and you will have elevated your bathroom to a new role of providing
pure pleasure...

But if, like many of us, you are stuck with more cramped
arrangements, read this book to see
how it's possible to organize storage,
create space and really add
character and style to any bathroom.

Introduction

Bathrooms are unique in the challenges they bring to the would-be decorator. To work well, they require generous-sized fittings sqeezed into one of the smallest rooms in the house. They have to be heated to a temperature that avoids goose-bumps in the nude, without creating such a steamy atmosphere that the towels are always damp. They need lighting which is soft enough to relax in at the end of a long day, but harsh enough to show up stubble and blemishes in the morning. They need power for razors, storage for all manner of bits and pieces, and the sort of plumbing that can always provide hot water for a long soak if required. Not only that, but they rely on one of the most dangerous combinations known to man: water and electricity.

ABOVE: HERE, THE STAINLESS STEEL BATH AND MATCHING TOILET ARE COMPLEMENTED BY THE CHROME FITTINGS AND SPARKLING CHANDELIER: A CONTEMPORARY TAKE ON TRADITIONAL DESIGN.

All in all, it's a tall order – but it is one that is well worth striving to get right – no matter how time-consuming.

THE RIGHT LOCATION

The first thing to consider is location. It is cheaper to redesign around an existing bathroom, but it may be that you want a bathroom that is closer to your bedroom or is larger in size. I certainly value having a bathroom-cum-dressing room next to my bedroom and dream one day of installing the bath in the bedroom itself. Perhaps you could increase the space available in your existing bathroom by locating the loo elsewhere. This is an admirable move, since the functions of defaecating and the pleasures of bathing seem at opposite ends of the spectrum. The only reason a loo is to be found in the bathroom at all is ease of plumbing; it really is better sited elsewhere. So spend some time just looking at the space you have got at your disposal – there is no rule book that says you must copy the existing location or layout. What matters is that the bathroom you design is right for your needs.

ABOVE: THE FINISHING TOUCH. CANDLELIGHT – HERE FROM SUITABLY WATER-LOVING CREATURES – BRINGS ROMANCE TO ANY BATHROOM.

Before you make a plan, write a bathroom checklist. This is to help you prioritize what you want. Ask yourself questions like:

• Is your present bathroom well located?

• Is your existing plumbing providing enough hot water?

• Will it still cope if you add a new fixture, such as a power shower?

• How does each member of the family use the bathroom (e.g. who showers and who bathes)?

• Do you need special safety provisions for children or elderly people (e.g. height of fixtures, shower thermostats, hard flooring, discreet handles)?

• How is the bathroom to be heated?

• How is it to be lit?

• Is a shaver socket outlet to be included?

• How much storage space do you have?

Some people use their bathroom for more than the obvious. They keep weights or exercise machines here. They store nappies, baby baths and other bulky items. They chuck their dirty clothes in the linen basket, pluck their eyebrows, dye their hair. They read magazines, drink wine, massage their loved ones. The choice is yours, but now is the time to think about what you want a bathroom for.

FINDING THE RIGHT PLUMBER

Everyone has plumber horror stories to tell, and certainly you should be guided by something more than cost. A good plumber is an engineer, craftsman and psychologist all rolled into one. He or she is there to help you plan the most intimate room in your home. Don't just hire the one that looks

BELOW: A BATHROOM NEEDN'T BE FILLED WITH DECORATIVE DETAILS. THIS SPARSE SCANDINAVIAN ROOM IS PURELY GIVEN OVER TO THE PRACTICALITIES.

the cheapest. Instead, it is fundamental that your plumber is reliable and always calls you back when you leave a message on the answering machine. This is important because almost certainly he or she will have to have a break in the job after the 'first fix' to allow the carpenter, tiler and painter in, leaving you to ring, maybe weeks later, to return for the 'second – and finishing – fix'.

You should also listen to other people's recommendations; ask to visit a previous client, and see the workmanship achieved. Also, make a mental note of how well maintained his or her vehicle looks, whether the

ABOVE: USE COLOUR TO ADD WARMTH TO A STARK BATHROOM – THE PANEL OF ORANGE MAKES THIS ENVIRONMENT CONSIDERABLY MORE ARRESTING.

plumber works with an assistant, and whether the business is VAT registered. All these things will provide clues as to the calibre of the person you are dealing with.

There are things a plumber will want from you too: a plan; catalogues of fixtures you are intending to use; the names of the electrician and builder you are planning to use and what sort of timetable you have agreed with them. Very importantly, your plumber will also want a written list of all the individual tasks that will make up the job, not just the plumbing, but a list of all the jobs for all the trades. This is a written specification (the 'spec'), and something that all the artisans should be issued with. As with kitchens, bathrooms can grind to a halt if one set of people is waiting for another lot to do their job, so try to keep them informed with any updates to the specification and even get them all together to agree what happens when.

You are also dependent on the manufacturer delivering on time. Again, keep everyone informed if they fail to do so. And finally, a useful tip: listen carefully to the plumber's comments when you first meet and revise your specifications if need be. Agree on a price and only renegotiate if it is fair to do so.

This is where all your hard work in planning the potentials and pre-empting the problems will pay dividends. The layout that you have worked so hard to design, and the written specification are the blueprints by which everyone else works, and once the bones are in place you can start to think of the surface details.

RIGHT: TO SOFTEN THE EFFECT STILL FURTHER CONSIDER COVERING OLD TILES WITH NEW, MORE BRIGHTLY COLOURED DESIGNS. PURPLE COMPLEMENTS ORANGE: THEY ARE BOTH SECONDARY COLOURS.

The *Makeovers*

Changing the design of your bathroom can mean anything from wallpapering the walls and making a new Roman blind for the window to installing the most up-to-date of bathroom suites, finishing the walls with a truly contemporary tinted plaster and laying a ceramic floor with mosaic insets. Whatever you favour, here are four makeovers that feature some of my favourite decorative devices.

The *Canopied* Bathroom

Sometimes an idea is not just a fixed thing but an evolving one. Even though the owners of this bathroom wanted a 'quick makeover', the scheme went through several incarnations before emerging as a sort of purple boudoir.

ABOVE: A DRAB AND DREARY SPACE, THIS BATHROOM REALLY NEEDED CHEERING UP.

A 'quick' makeover, this space had several obvious problems. The ceiling was disproportionately high for the room; the previous owners had tried to solve this by tiling to shoulder height. This made the place feel like a public lavatory. The colours were also cold, the floor uninteresting, and the toilet was right next to the bath. Very unsatisfactory.

Initially, the solution lay in a black and white scheme, lowering the tiles and 'losing' the ceiling in white. Accessories would be chrome. Very 1930s, and very stylish. But the ceiling idea just wouldn't work in such a small space.

We really needed to bring it down, and the best way to do this optically was with a warm, advancing colour like red, or orange. But why not bring the colour down the wall too, to drag the ceiling down even further? Brilliant! The canopy idea was born, still in a decorative 1930s vein. Furthermore, since black, white and orange seemed a rather severe combination, the colour purple sprang to mind as an almost obvious choice for down below. The whole room was re-decorated, including flooring and tiles, for less than £1000.

ABOVE: WHEN COMPARED
TO THE BEFORE PICTURE
(OPPOSITE), THE FINISHED
BATHROOM APPEARS
MUCH MORE INTIMATE
AND LUXURIOUS.

Tiling

The idea of purple tiles instead of black seemed much more exciting and unusual, and not without cause, because it took several days of detective work to find even one manufacturer who made a purple tile. Eventually we found two. The final choice of which was a purple tile with a deep transparent glaze, much more interesting (if twice the price) than a thin, machine-made tile with a very flat and opaque glaze, as it looked more like paint. The effort and cost was worth it, however, because the effect is scintillating and the uneven surface of each tile gives the overall impression of a room that has been 'quilted'.

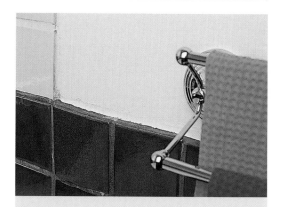

ABOVE: WE TILED ONTO THE OLD TILES EXCEPT AROUND THE SHOWER, WHERE THE WHITE TILES WENT STRAIGHT ONTO THE WALL ABOVE THE PURPLE, PRODUCING A CLEAR 'STEP' WHERE THE PURPLE DADO MEETS THE WHITE WALL.

1 *Work out your dry run with dry tiles to test the effect. Ensure the walls are straight and corners flush. If not, build up with timber or plaster and then stick the tiles with the adhesive.*

2 *To cut a tile, score the surface with the cutter and snap the tile gently over an edge. Handmade tiles will fail more often than machine-made ones so allow at least 10 per cent extra tiles for tricky jobs.*

3 *Use a carborundum to smooth cut edges, or use coarse wet and dry paper. Curved edges can be cut away with a 'nibbler' and then smoothed. Finish with the waterproof grout.*

ABOVE AND RIGHT: THE OLD
SCHEME WAS SO WEAK THAT THE
TILES REQUIRED A MOULDING AND
LINE TO CAP THEM. THIS IS A
FUSSY HANGOVER FROM COMPLEX
VICTORIAN SCHEMES. THE
STRENGTH OF OUR ROOM STEMS
FROM THE USE OF STRONG,
CLEAR BLOCKS OF COLOUR.

Stencilling

I have always maintained that stencilling is not really an art form in itself (though its great practitioners today have elevated it to that position), but simply a means to an end, a pattern made to help the painter produce something else, or at best, an early form of printing. Stencils were used by the Egyptians for their hieroglyphics and I have worked with a French illustrator who is perhaps the only remaining practitioner of medieval stencilling, as used to create multiple illuminated manuscripts. In both these cases, it is impossible to tell from the finished work that a stencil was ever used. That's exactly the principle we set out to follow in this room.

The block of purple at the bottom of the room is solid and simply defined. Consequently, I felt a little uneasy about just painting the ceiling in another flat block of orange. Although effective in visually lowering the ceiling, it would have seemed a bit obvious and rather ungainly. The solution we found was to treat it in a decorative way, but it was important that the result shouldn't look fussy and spoil the room's strengths and the effect of the advancing colour. As a result, we went for a very graphic treatment, choosing a hanging tassel design that brought the orange down the walls and therefore lowered the ceiling even further, while implying a sort of decorative, exotic tent (a very 1920s or

1930s image). To keep it simple, the tassels were only painted in silhouette and given a very crisp edge by freehand painting after the stencilling. As a result, it was impossible to tell that the design had ever been stencilled at all.

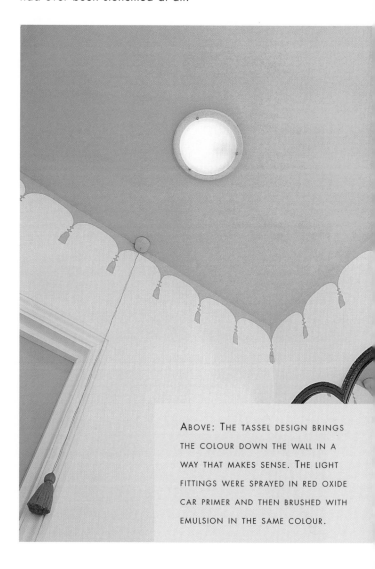

ABOVE: THE TASSEL DESIGN BRINGS THE COLOUR DOWN THE WALL IN A WAY THAT MAKES SENSE. THE LIGHT FITTINGS WERE SPRAYED IN RED OXIDE CAR PRIMER AND THEN BRUSHED WITH EMULSION IN THE SAME COLOUR.

CUTTING AND USING THE STENCIL

1 Offer a piece of paper up to the area in which your design will appear on the wall and roughly sketch out proportions. Finish the design on the table.

2 Cut out the shape with scissors to make a template. Remember to cut or mark the points where the design repeats or makes contact with features in the room, such as the ceiling.

3 Carefully draw around the template to transfer the design onto a sheet of stencil card. Alternatively, you may prefer just to stick down the design before the next stage.

4 Using the scalpel or craft knife, cut out the stencil (use scissors for large areas). Put a cutting mat underneath and work slowly rather than applying strong pressure.

5 Using the stencil brush (if you have one – I always use a stiff decorating brush) stipple on the colour. You need to put very little paint on the brush. Remove the stencil.

6 When dry, outline the design carefully with a fine artist's brush. Although it needs care, you can complete this step remarkably quickly, and the result is excellent.

YOU WILL NEED ... Paper • Pencil • Scissors • Sharp scalpel or craft knife • Stencil card • Scissors • Cutting mat • A stencil brush or stiff, short-bristled brush for stencilling • Paint • Artist's sable brush for outlining

TIP

To make your own stencil card, coat a sheet of thin card on both sides with boiled linseed oil and allow to dry for a few days. This will make it both waterproof and much tougher.

Spraying the soap baskets

The canopy design and the use of intense colours in this room suggested a sort of quirkiness, as though the room has a sense of humour. I really felt we could exploit that further and introduce accessories that said the same thing. Moreover, as an alternative to a huge bathroom cupboard, we felt that many of the lotions and potions could go on view, rather than piling them high on a precarious windowsill. So we chose an assortment of little trays and cages that could be fixed to the wall.

They were arranged around the room so that they punctuated the walls rather like a series of full stops. The deliberate choice of different colours was used to soften the hard edge of the purple tiles.

WIRE BASKETS

These wire items are the kind of thing on sale in high street stores, made in the Far East and imported with a galvanized steel finish for use in bathrooms and kitchens. Their look, if anything, is rustic, belonging in the farmhouse kitchen or a Conran bathroom. However, by spraying them with intensely coloured paints, their character changes completely into something that is much more in keeping with this room. I find that metallic or pearlescent car paints are excellent for this kind of work.

> YOU WILL NEED ...
> Dust mask • Red oxide car spray primer (other coloured primers will do) • Car spray paints or decorative spray paints

1 Although, strictly speaking, paint will not adhere to galvanized (zinc-coated) steel, in practice red oxide primer will stick well enough for non-industrial purposes.

2 When dry, apply the first coloured top coat, spraying over old newspaper. Aim the nozzle at the basket, but not too near. To recoat, turn the object when dry.

3 Carefully spray a second and even third colour on the object, directing the spray carefully to avoid too much blending. Respray the first colour as necessary.

ABOVE: I THOUGHT ORIGINALLY OF PAINTING SOME 1930S RETRO DEVICES AROUND THE ROOM ABOVE THE TILES, BUT THE PAINTED BASKETS ARE ALTOGETHER MORE WACKY AND PRACTICAL.

Surfaces

The bathroom has to be practical, of course, but there are subtler themes to follow if we also want this space to be a relaxing environment. A sense of luxury is essential and you won't get it if you don't balance your surfaces and textures. We balanced the hard glossiness of the tiles by using a dead flat emulsion paint on the walls and ceilings, continuing that softness onto the light fittings, which were painted matt orange and came with matt, sandblasted glass. Because we didn't intend to hang curtains, it was important to soften the room in other ways. A blind helped, but we achieved what we wanted mainly with the lighting, installing two bowls on the ceiling and controlling them with a dimmer. Towels and bathmats in contrasting colours to the tiles also help; they seem highlighted against the deep purple and draw the eye with their contrasting texture.

LEFT: THIS SCREEN IS STRATEGICALLY PLACED BETWEEN THE TOILET PAN AND THE PLACE WHERE YOUR HEAD RESTS IN THE BATH. IT IS A SIMPLE BUT EFFECTIVE IDEA THAT HAS BEEN TIED INTO THE SCHEME WITH PURPLE PAINT AND TWO COATS OF GLOSS VARNISH.

TIP

Plan your arrangement of textures and surfaces with sample tiles, flooring, paint and even towels beforehand. Aim for juxtapositions that are interesting, stimulating or suggest luxury.

FINE FLOORING

We originally intended to lay a purple carpet in the room, again to soften the hardness of the tiles, but also to continue the purple underfoot and to suggest a supportive 'cradle' of colour at the bottom of the room. However, the final choice was a vinyl tile flooring, which is slightly textured and has a translucent quality with a purple metallic sheen; quite seductive, very luxurious and totally unexpected.

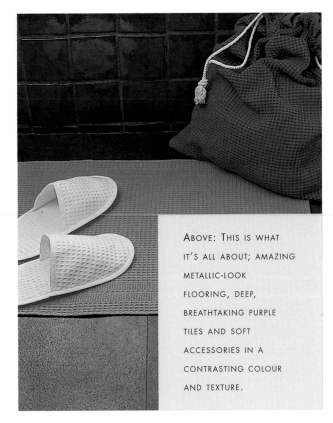

ABOVE: THIS MIRROR FROM A JUNK SHOP WAS A 'MUST-HAVE'. IT WAS PAINTED PURPLE BY THE OWNERS TO MATCH THE REST OF THE DECOR.

ABOVE: THIS IS WHAT IT'S ALL ABOUT; AMAZING METALLIC-LOOK FLOORING, DEEP, BREATHTAKING PURPLE TILES AND SOFT ACCESSORIES IN A CONTRASTING COLOUR AND TEXTURE.

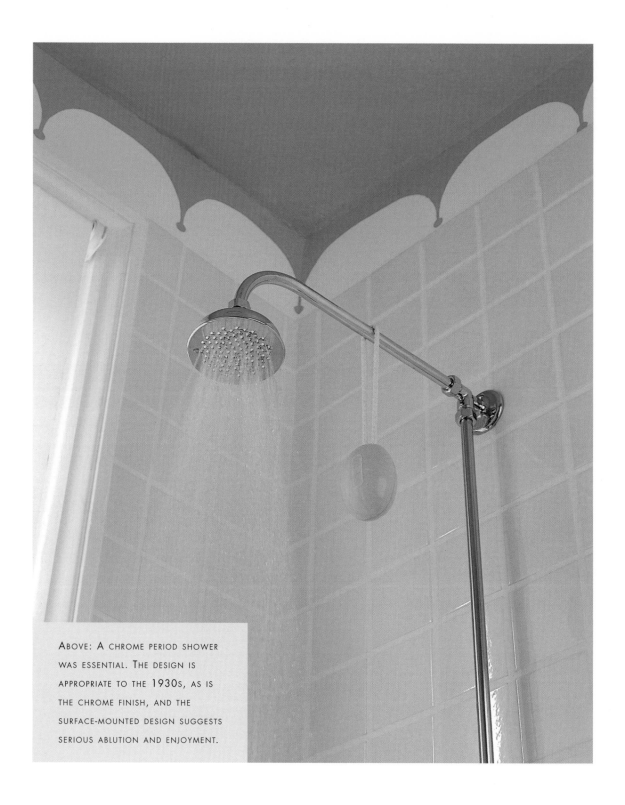

ABOVE: A CHROME PERIOD SHOWER WAS ESSENTIAL. THE DESIGN IS APPROPRIATE TO THE 1930S, AS IS THE CHROME FINISH, AND THE SURFACE-MOUNTED DESIGN SUGGESTS SERIOUS ABLUTION AND ENJOYMENT.

Details and Accessories

Just because a space is small, it doesn't mean that you can get away with not 'propping' it at all. A minimal look is usually less to do with quantity than the quality and appropriateness of the fittings. Although this bathroom was small, or rather because it was small, we had to make sure that everything worked, matched or fitted perfectly. That's why I spent so much time getting the colour of the wire trays right, rather than just plonking them on the wall in their original galvanized finish. It's usually in the details that a room 'comes together' and because they hold such importance they should be conceptualized as part of the room, before you decorate. Work out your colours, patterns and basic design, and then add styling details in your mind.

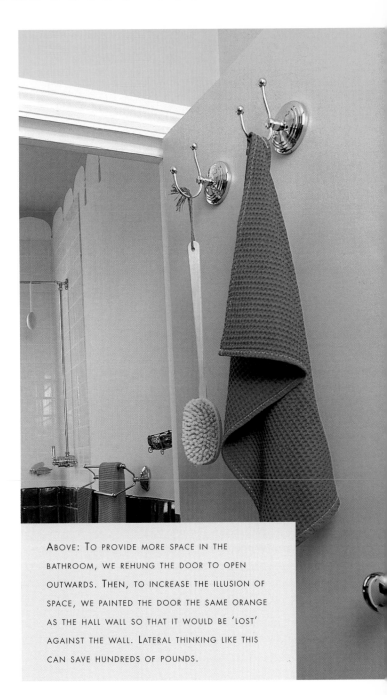

LEFT: LITTLE DETAILS LIKE ORANGE TASSELS FOR THE BLIND AND LIGHT PULL-SWITCH, WHICH TIE IN WITH THE STENCILLED CEILING, SHOW THAT THOUGHT AND CARE HAVE GONE INTO A SCHEME. NOTE HOW THE WINDOW FRAME CARRIES THE PURPLE LINE AROUND THE ROOM IN PAINT.

ABOVE: TO PROVIDE MORE SPACE IN THE BATHROOM, WE REHUNG THE DOOR TO OPEN OUTWARDS. THEN, TO INCREASE THE ILLUSION OF SPACE, WE PAINTED THE DOOR THE SAME ORANGE AS THE HALL WALL SO THAT IT WOULD BE 'LOST' AGAINST THE WALL. LATERAL THINKING LIKE THIS CAN SAVE HUNDREDS OF POUNDS.

The *Hedonist's* Bathroom

Contemporary design in a bathroom is not just about using up-to-the-minute fixtures. It is also about surface finish, the need to create space, simplicity of layout and attention to detail.

On first acquaintance, this bathroom presented a combination of unsavoury colours and surfaces, and the sink, bath and cupboard stuck out into the room like great unyielding lumps of masonry. The brief was to establish an atmosphere of understated luxury with an exacting level of finish. When starting to make our plans, we consulted the builder, Martin, about the layout of the room. A few big decisions resulted: to remove the tatty cornice, and to 'shrink' the boiler cupboard (on the left in the photograph opposite) to provide space for a newly-positioned bath. The biggest step, however, was to move out the partition wall in which the door was sited by 18 cm (7 in) to provide just enough space for a walk-in shower. An excellent finishing touch. Of course, all this work made for an expensive piece of interior design, but as it was a long-term solution the owners felt it was money well spent.

RIGHT: RATHER THAN BOX IN THE BATH AND CREATE YET ANOTHER LARGE LUMP IN THE ROOM, A FREE-STANDING VERSION WAS CHOSEN TO CONTRIBUTE TO THE FEELING OF SPACE IN THE BATHROOM.

Design Principles

To give a sense of space to any room, the first thing to do is get rid of the clutter: not just the paraphernalia of life but the fussy architectural detailing as well. We eliminated the cornice, shrank the cupboard on the left, and replaced the louvred doors and architraves with a very simple unpanelled door. This kind of process clears the decks for the introduction of bold statements which otherwise would appear to be too compromised and weakened by there being so much around, distracting the eye. I suppose that the trendy word for this simplified, bold approach is 'graphic'. Some might even say 'architectural'. The point is that it requires just as much care and thought as a more complex decorative scheme.

ABOVE AND BELOW: THE WHITE FEET WERE A NICE TOUCH – SPILLING THE COLOUR OF THE CERAMIC ONTO THE OUTSIDE OF THE BATH AND ACTING AS A BUFFER BETWEEN ALL THE SECONDARY COLOURS.

The bath

As the bath is a symbol of luxurious pampering, it had to take centre stage in this room. We discussed placing it in the middle of the room, but by moving back the cupboard on the left, and treating it with the same wall finish as the rest of the room, we managed to provide an important space for the bath against the back wall. A bath is a big item of furniture by any room's standard, and so it was not surprising that having got its position right, everything else in the room slotted into place.

The next trick to provide the bath with an assertive grandeur was to paint it a contrasting colour. Orange became the obvious choice, since it is the third secondary colour in the spectrum – and we already had introduced the other two to the bathroom, green and purple. The colour served another useful purpose – since orange appeared so alien to the 'period' look of the bath, it helped link the bath to its very contemporary environment.

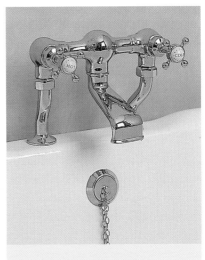

ABOVE: ALTHOUGH THESE REPRODUCTION TAPS ARE NOT AWE-INSPIRINGLY MODERN, ANYTHING ELSE ON THIS TRADITIONAL-STYLE BATH WOULD HAVE APPEARED RIDICULOUS.

1 On a rusting bath remove any old or loose paint with a wire brush and coat with a water-borne rust 'converter' to turn it to magnatite.

2 Rust converters can be painted over within a few hours. Use a red oxide primer/undercoat – a water-borne acrylic one is perfect.

3 Apply two coats of emulsion paint, and finish with two coats of matt acrylic varnish when dry.

YOU WILL NEED ... *Stiff wire brush • Water-borne rust 'converter' (available from a car accessories shop) • Red oxide acrylic primer/undercoat • Paintbrush • Acrylic paint • Matt acrylic varnish*

The walls

The maxim still holds that, 'the quickest way to change a room is with a can of coloured paint'. Only in this bathroom, we didn't use paint, but tinted plaster with a thin wash of colour over the top. Admittedly, we could perhaps have just colourwashed these walls with a green paint using the technique used in the Portuguese bathroom on pages 46-7, but the qualities of tinted plaster are quite unlike that of paint. Rather, plaster has a perceptible translucency because it is not nearly as opaque as paint. As a consequence, the colour appears to be 'in' it and the surface takes on all the imperfections, dots of unmixed pigment, impurities and marks left by the 'polish' of the trowel, as plasterers call this final pass. Of course, it is not a technique that you should rush and try by yourself – it really requires the assistance of a very competent, and very compliant, plasterer. Be prepared to pay for any time spent helping you with colour samples. This process, essential and not a little laborious, is the one we show opposite, and bear in mind that even the finished colours of your samples can vary depending how you treat your walls: with varnish, thinned PVA, or

RIGHT: COMBINING DIFFERENT LIGHTING SOURCES WITH WALLS LIKE THESE REALLY BRINGS OUT THE SUBTLE SURFACE QUALITIES OF THE PLASTER.

TESTING FOR COLOUR

YOU WILL NEED ...
For the trial: Pigment (preferably in powder form as liquid stainers may prevent plaster from drying) • *Small paintbrushes* • *White all-in-one plaster* • *Flexible bucket* • *Mixing pots and sticks* • *Sample plasterboard* • *Trowel*

1 *Whether you use pigment in powder or liquid form, mix it with water first to form a loose, liquidy paste. Use a brush to 'grind' and mix the pigment until it has dissolved.*

2 *Mix up a quantity of plaster in the bucket and mix equal quantities into the different pigment mixes. Stir well and trowel onto the plasterboard.*

TIP

Sampling like this is essential to get the colour right. To ensure that the finished wall matches your sample, measure all your quantities scrupulously and multiply up when mixing the real thing.

3 *I used three different strengths of the same pigment, viridian, to produce three very different greens, carefully measuring the quantities of the ingredients.*

4 *Beware! As it dries, the plaster 'comes through' the colour, rendering it much paler. You must allow the plaster samples to dry for 24 hours before making a judgement about the colour.*

even beeswax polish. However you intend to finish the walls, do always seal the plastered surface with at least three coats of dilute PVA first.

As a luxurious alternative to all this, you could always call on one of the handful of specialist companies who do this kind of work, which is now becoming increasingly popular.

For a highly glossy finish that is redolent of marble, you could specify *stucco lustro*, or *stucco Veneziano*, as it is sometimes called, a form of gesso made with glue, chalk and powdered marble dust which is thinly trowelled onto the walls and then laboriously polished when dry. This is an expensive finish, but it is beautiful and durable.

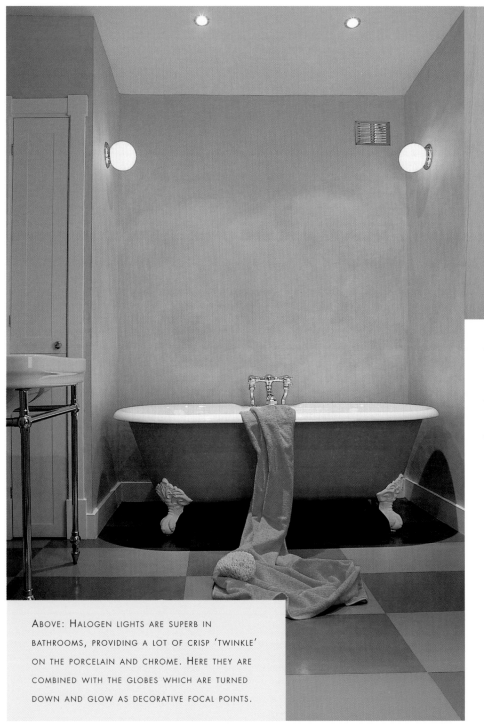

ABOVE: THESE EXCELLENT MIRROR LIGHTS TAKE LOW-WATTAGE TUNGSTEN BULBS WHICH TOGETHER PRODUCE NO GLARE AND A SHADOWLESS, OVERALL BRIGHT LIGHT FOR PUTTING ON MAKE-UP OR FOR SHAVING.

ABOVE: HALOGEN LIGHTS ARE SUPERB IN BATHROOMS, PROVIDING A LOT OF CRISP 'TWINKLE' ON THE PORCELAIN AND CHROME. HERE THEY ARE COMBINED WITH THE GLOBES WHICH ARE TURNED DOWN AND GLOW AS DECORATIVE FOCAL POINTS.

Lighting Effects

The bathroom is not the first room for which you might consider a lighting scheme. Yet why not? It is surely the most diverse of rooms, the only place where a host of human activities is crammed into the smallest of spaces. We shave, dress, coiffe, clean, and even doze there. We also, amazingly, use the room for both relaxing and for re-vitalizing ourselves. Little wonder that we ought to light bathrooms with a flexible lighting system.

This room's lighting has actually been designed in a very simple way and is connected to two circuits, each on a dimmer controlled from outside the door. One circuit feeds the four low-voltage downlighters in the ceiling, and the other feeds two tungsten globe lights on the walls above the bath. The mirror lights are fitted with their own switch.

RIGHT: WHEN THE HALOGEN BULBS ARE EXTINGUISHED AND THE GLOBES TURNED UP, YOU HAVE THE PERFECT LIGHT TO RELAX BY; AN OVERALL WARM, EVEN, GENTLE FLOOD OF LIGHT.

Fittings

If God is in the detail, then so is the Devil. The finished room may be spare, but in such minimal circumstances, every tiny element comes under scrutiny. A more expansive and decorative scheme is an easy structure in which to hide things: faults or junk. This room, however, has no dark corners to conceal such easy and sham solutions. Little details matter hugely in such circumstances – for example, all the screw heads used for fixings around the room had to be slot-headed and finished in chrome or stainless steel.

ABOVE: THE WINDOW TREATMENT IS SUPERB. OUT WENT THE CURTAINS AND IN CAME SANDBLASTED GLASS FOR A VERY CHIC, MATT EFFECT.

BELOW: BEFORE THE MAKEOVER. LUCKILY, THE LOO HOVERS IN ITS OWN CRANNY, OUT OF THE WAY OF THE REST OF THE ROOM.

THAT SINKING FEELING

The porcelain details around the room have all taken their lead from the bath, and so reflect the traditional, while at the same time conveying something of the contemporary about them. As a celebration of the functional, the toilet cistern is exposed and the pan changed for a more assertive Edwardian repro design. The basin, traditional in plan, is mounted on a rather sophisticated stand that establishes chrome as the secondary material in this bathroom. There's lots of it around the room, found in details like bath hooks, handles and the superb lighting fixtures which are certified for use in bathrooms (few are). The trick to the simplicity of design in this room is the combination of attention to detail, time-proven materials for the rather sexy hardware and use of pretty strong colour.

ABOVE: THIS RADIATOR COMBINES THE ESSENCE OF THE DESIGN IDEAS IN THIS ROOM. THE FINISH IS HIGH GLOSS ENAMEL AND THE DESIGN TRADITIONAL, BUT IT IS A LOW-PROFILE MODERN EXAMPLE.

LEFT: THE SHEER VOLUME OF CHROME IN THE ROOM CREATES A VERY STREAMLINED AND EFFICIENT IMAGE. RATHER THAN APPEARING INDUSTRIAL, LIKE BRUSHED STAINLESS STEEL, CHROME SUGGESTS THE GRAND PLUMBING ARRANGEMENTS OF THE 1930S.

The Flooring

LEFT: RUBBER FLOORING HAS MANY GREAT ATTRIBUTES. IT IS WARM UNDERFOOT, SOFT, SPRINGY, AND – BEST OF ALL – WATERPROOF.

Getting the flooring right was a big coup. Because it is the surface on which all the room's hardware sits, the floor has to suggest solidity and mass, something not possible with stained pine boards or carpet. My first choice was this synthetic rubber, made in France and available in myriad colours. A chequerboard suggested itself, simply in order to provide a jaunty feeling – a sort of Disneyesque floor on which you felt the bath could almost spring into life and jive its way out of the corner. Usefully, this flooring is available in large 'double tiles', providing the opportunity for an altogether more interesting check pattern. We tiled the floor onto waterproof board.

The Shower

Carving a space for the shower was not easy and ultimately meant moving the partition wall out onto the landing to make room. This helped enormously because the wall to the side of the shower consists of a chimney breast, against which, on either side, cupboards had been built to project forwards. Because of the breast and alcove arrangement, these cupboards were very deep, providing just the space for a large and impressive shower.

LEFT: BEFORE, THE BATHROOM SEEMED CRAMPED AND MESSY. THERE WAS TOO MUCH IN TOO SMALL A SPACE; OUT WENT THE WASHING MACHINE FOR A START.

LEFT: THE FINISHED SHOWER. I'M NOT TOO COMFORTABLE ABOUT DELVING INTO THE PSYCHOLOGY OF WHY MEN GENERALLY PREFER SHOWERS TO BATHS, AND WOMEN VICE VERSA. IT IS NEEDLESS TO ASK WHO WANTED THIS LUXURIOUS ARRANGEMENT OF BODY-PUMMELLING DELUGES!

The obvious solution to decorating a small space is to go for a simple, uncluttered scheme, to add airiness. But the solution in this case was to go the other way, by adding more, and yet more, decoration and detail.

The *Portuguese* Bathroom

The clients for this bathroom were very particular. They wanted to convert a rather dingy and extremely small bathroom on the landing of a Georgian house into something that, well, represented something of a fantasy for them: a space that would remind them of their holidays to northern Portugal. Easy,

you might think. But, in reality, it posed several problems.

The first was how to shoehorn in all the plumbing and sanitary ware, given that they wanted a bigger bath, much larger basin and a shower. A more aesthetic – and more demanding – problem, however, was how to get the decoration right using Portuguese tiles, without it looking like an effort tastelessly thrown together in the 1960s!

To create a bathroom like this would cost less than £1000 if the fittings weren't to be replaced.

LEFT: WHEN I FIRST SAW THIS BATHROOM, IT LOOKED SAD AND UNLOVED, THE PLASTIC BATH WAS TOO SMALL, AND THAT COLOUR – PAMPAS – JUST HAD TO GO...

BELOW: THE END RESULT. THE BATH TAPS ARE MOUNTED ON THE WALL SO I ASKED FOR THE BATH TO BE DELIVERED WITHOUT THE TAP HOLES BEING PRE-DRILLED. YOUR INSTALLER COULD DRILL THEM FOR YOU IF NECESSARY.

Authenticity and detail

LEFT: DETAILS MATTER, LIKE THE MDF SHAPE JIG-SAWED OUT AND SET INTO THE TILES AT THE BACK OF THE CISTERN, GIVING THE WATERWORKS A SENSE OF GRAND PURPOSE. ALSO, THE SURFACE ON EACH SIDE OF THE LOO HAS BEEN MADE REMOVABLE FOR ACCESS (TILING GROUT CAN COVER THE JOINT — AND WILL BREAK EASILY).

BOXING IN

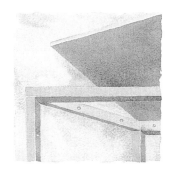

1 Create a wooden frame, screwing it to the wall wherever possible. Then cut pieces of plywood to fit the top and front (and sides, if necessary for your bathroom) and screw in place.

RIGHT: THE BAROQUE CURVE ON THIS WALL WAS MADE BY SCORING CHUNKS OFF THE TILES WITH A CUTTER, THEN NIBBLING THEM WITH PINCERS AND SANDING THE EDGES WITH CARBORUNDUM PAPER FOR A SMOOTH FINISH.

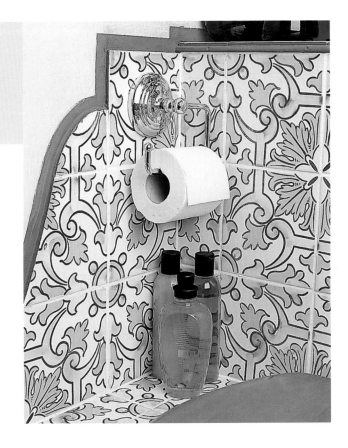

To give a truly Portuguese look to the room, it was pretty clear we had to use traditional Portuguese tiles with a strong baroque design, and these we found from a British importer. However, it wasn't all that easy, as you can find out on page 44. But to avoid that ghastly 1960s feel, it was also necessary to concentrate on the details. I chose seagrass flooring, and there were subtle things we could do like boxing in the toilet pan to suggest a Mediterranean or even Arab 'bench', or adding curves and strong baroque scrolls to the design.

2 The surface on either side of the loo was made in two pieces. Make cardboard templates to fit in the spaces and draw around them on the plywood. Use a jigsaw to cut them out.

3 Plywood is an especially good surface for tiling onto. Before sticking the tiles, lay them out to ensure they match with the least number of cuts and their repeats are kept reasonably continuous.

YOU WILL NEED ...
5 x 2.5 cm (2 x 1 in) timber for frame • Screws • Screwdriver • Drill and drill bits • Plywood • Saw • Pencil • Cardboard • Scissors • Jigsaw • Tiles • Tile adhesive • Spreader • Grout

Fitting it all in

The big practical challenge in this room was how to get the new fixtures to fit the space. The room isn't wide but we were just able to accommodate a slightly larger bath (the old bath's panel stuck out an extra 5 cm [2 in]!). The far end wall is an exterior one, so it was considered unwise to place the shower feed pipes in that wall because of the freezing risk. So, somewhat unconventionally, the power shower was attached on the side wall.

SPACE ENHANCING

Luckily, the old basin positively luxuriated in space, allowing us to shunt it into the corner, making a little more room for that longer bath, but still allowing us to replace it with an altogether larger, and nicer, vanity basin. The chance to devise a vanity unit, although more expensive, is a godsend. In a trice, you can place the basin at your preferred height, provide storage, and give a useful surface. This one also houses the shower pump.

ABOVE: THE ROOM IS SMALL, BUT SO IS THE DOOR, SO THE VANITY UNIT CAN BE LARGE ENOUGH TO HOUSE A REALLY DECENT-SIZED BASIN.

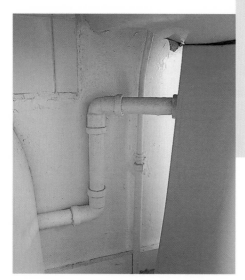

LEFT: THOSE FEW VITAL CENTIMETRES OF SPACE BETWEEN THE BATH AND SINK MEANT THAT A LONGER BATH COULD BE INSTALLED.

TIP

Remember that others have been before you. In this case, I spent two hours and several sheets of graph paper before realizing that there was only one possible layout for this room – the one that was already there!

LEFT: THE RESULT IS A TRIUMPH (IF A BASIN EVER COULD BE SUCH A THING), WITH A USEFUL BASIN SET ON A GENEROUS SLAB OF CARRARA MARBLE (COURTESY OF THE LOCAL MONUMENTAL MASONS). THE LARGE MIRROR BEHIND THE BASIN MAKES THE ROOM FEEL BIGGER.

Painting the tiles

The real secret to the visual success of this bathroom is, without doubt, the tiling. The problem was that the border tiles to go with the pattern just weren't in the country, and of course, being August, the Portuguese factory was closed. The less-than-obvious alternative was to paint our own, a good weekend's work, but worth it. I used low-firing ceramic paints that can be fired in an oven, and although this was my first attempt, the results are quite satisfactory. This was despite the fact that when the colours were diluted to watercolour thinness, the resultant glaze was less stable in parts after firing. However, a pleasantly random unevenness of colour was produced.

THINK BIG

Another sound principle with a baroque scheme such as this one is to make the scale big and expansive. With this in mind, we made the frames for the tile panels around the mirror each a whole tile wide, and with a strong, slightly three-dimensional, moulded, trompe l'œil effect.

YOU WILL NEED ...
A large flat work surface • Plain tiles • Methylated spirits • Pencil or pen • Ruler or straight edge • Soft brushes • Water • Ceramic paints in pots and squeezy tubes for fine line work • Masking tape • Hot oven (read instructions that come with the paints)

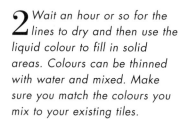

1 Clean the tiles with methylated spirits, lay three or four of them out in a row and mark out the line work if necessary with the pencil and ruler. Follow the lines with a squeezy tube of colour, laying it against the straight edge.

2 Wait an hour or so for the lines to dry and then use the liquid colour to fill in solid areas. Colours can be thinned with water and mixed. Make sure you match the colours you mix to your existing tiles.

3 Cook! – following the manufacturer's instructions exactly. Because the colours can change during firing (particularly when thinned, as I found out), do a test tile first. Allow it to cool and if you are happy with it, tile your wall.

LEFT: THE RESULTS CAN BE VERY IMPRESSIVE, ADDING REAL DECORATIVE WEIGHT AND AN HISTORICAL OR REGIONAL ACCURACY TO YOUR DECORATING. TO HELP ME, I RESEARCHED THE PATTERNS LOOKING AT EIGHTEENTH-CENTURY PORTUGUESE EXAMPLES IN A LIBRARY BOOK.

ABOVE: TO BE EVEN MORE QUIRKY (AS IS THE CASE IN PORTUGAL), I USED TWO DIFFERENT FRAME DESIGNS NEXT TO EACH OTHER. THE MACHINE-MADE INFILL TILES ON THE LEFT NOW LOOK STUNNING — AS THOUGH THEY HAD BEEN HAND-PAINTED AS WELL.

Getting the walls right

If this were a true Portuguese bathroom, the walls would perhaps be painted white, or papered with a mad fake-tile wallpaper. But as this particular bathroom is in England, the client really wanted something much warmer. So the obvious option was a much more Italian colour – in this case yellow ochre – which exudes the essence of the Mediterranean and even in a north-facing room retains its charm and warmth. It is the only yellow pigment that really works in northern climates because it will, luckily, never appear cold and greenish. And it is truly universal, belonging just as happily in limewashes in this country as in Florence.

As a solid paint, yellow ochre is just too heavy and indigestible. It needs either diluting with white or, as in this case, colourwashing onto the wall and then coated with an incredibly thin coat of white paint to 'dust' it, giving an effect of dry plaster.

MAKING THE PREPARATIONS

The paint I used was one made up in the container from matt acrylic varnish (water-based and very tough) diluted one part paint to seven or eight parts water, and with yellow ochre powder pigment added at the early mixing stage. We were able to get a very soft effect by thorough reparation of the ground. We then lined the walls, filled the cracks and emulsioned, before sanding smooth and coating with two coats of thinned satin acrylic varnish. This gave the walls 'slip' so necessary to aid colourwashing.

ABOVE: TO REALLY WARM UP THE ROOM, WE CARRIED THE COLOURWASHING OVER THE CEILING. AS A RESULT, THE FACT THAT IT IS SLOPING IS SOMEWHAT LOST.

TIP

When colourwashing with water-based paints, avoid hard painted edges by extending the working time of the paint. Either damp the walls with a sponge first or leave bowls of water in the room overnight. In a bathroom, you could always just turn the shower on; the effect is just as good.

COLOURWASHING

1 To make a good colourwash mix yourself, either thin down emulsion paint (1 part paint to 6 parts water), or (for a bathroom) mix acrylic varnish with artist's acrylic colours (a bit expensive but they go a long way) or pigment. We used 2 tablespoons of pigment to about half a cup of varnish.

YOU WILL NEED ...
Emulsion paint or matt water-borne acrylic varnish with artist's acrylic colours • Large containers • Large decorating brush • Softener brush • White emulsion • Matt varnish • Rags

2 Once the pigment and varnish are mixed well (you may need water to help), thin to a skimmed milk consistency and brush out quickly.

3 This is the hard bit. The paint quickly begins to stick to the brush. Deliberately make coarse patterns, or soften with the softener paintbrush.

4 A few minutes later, using the softener, pass lightly over the surface of the wall in all directions, quickly removing visible brushstrokes.

DUSTING

1 I also call this veiling. Dilute some white emulsion, 1 part paint to 8 or 10 parts water, and add 1 or 2 parts matt varnish. This will render it tough and quite waterproof.

2 Lightly and very quickly brush it out over the wall. You may wish to dampen the wall with a sponge first to help keep the paint from drying too quickly at this stage.

3 Immediately dry the brush on a rag and very lightly, tickling in fact, soften the surface in all directions. Don't overdo it – the dampness will blur the brushmarks together.

The Window Detail

The window in this room presented us with a problem as it is small, recessed and provides precious little light. It was also in the wrong place as we needed a little extra space to provide the tiled splashback for the shower. In the end, we built a new false reveal on the right-hand side at 90 degrees to the window (see page 39 where the end result is clear for all to admire), while the left reveal remains as it was, slightly angled. No one has noticed yet ...

ABOVE: THE WINDOW SILL WAS ORIGINALLY CLUMSILY MASKED BY THE CISTERN AND A CHEAP TILED UPSTAND. WE TIDIED THIS UP AS SHOWN ON PAGES 40-1.

LEFT: NO PORTUGUESE WINDOW IS COMPLETE WITHOUT A SHUTTER. THIS ONE IS FROM A DIY STORE AND I BURNT THE SHUTTER WITH A BLOWTORCH TO RAISE THE GRAIN BEFORE PAINTING WITH BLUE ACRYLIC.

Finishing Touches

The problem with tiling a room in an old house is that the walls are guaranteed not to be straight. Come to that, they rarely are in a new house, and tiles have a nasty habit of coming with very square corners. A good tiler can make up for all sorts of deficiencies in a room, but every man has his limit; and this room set that limit very clearly. The wall to the right of the basin was outrageously slanted. Paint was the much more fluid solution, and we applied it in the form of a dark blue line taken round the tiles, and so as not to highlight our dreadful wall, also round the whole room at the tiles' edge.

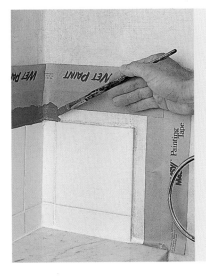

LEFT: THE BLUE LINE, CHOSEN TO MATCH THE BLUE IN THE TILES, WAS PAINTED WITH A LONG BRUSH, USING ACRYLIC PAINT. A REALLY CRISP EFFECT CAN BE OBTAINED WITH MASKING TAPE.

I find it intriguing that rooms that have complicated decorative schemes are ever hungry for more decoration. Once you have decided upon an elaborate design, it always seems to me that in order to build a satisfying effect, you must add threefold the quantity of what you originally planned in terms of accessories and details. It is almost as though we have forgotten how to design complex interiors.

LEFT: AS WELL AS A LANTERN IN THE ROOM, THIS MDF PELMET (CUT TO A TEMPLATE AND PAINTED TO MATCH THE WALLS) WAS FIXED TO CONCEAL A RECESSED LOW-VOLTAGE SPOTLIGHT ABOVE THE SINK. THE RESULT IS PERFECT AMBIENT LIGHT IN FRONT OF THE MIRROR.

▼ TIP

Instead of buying cheap, and somewhat useless masking tape, get hold of the brown paper 'easy-mask' variety. It will not remove paint or even wallpaper and gives a faultless edge.

The *Toile* Toilet

The smallest room in the house often merits the most lavish attention to detail. After all, every square inch will come under scrutiny for long stretches at a time.

This very traditional room is an especial favourite of mine for two reasons. First, I have wanted to do something with shells indoors for a long time. Second, this room is in our house.

It may be super trad, but it wins admiring looks from anyone spending any time sitting in it. What more could one ask? Such a room can demand the uninterrupted attention of a captive audience, and (especially important, this), because of its size, merits your spending a little more time on its decoration. This principle extends to the details and accessories as well. As pointed out elsewhere in this book, the smaller the space and the longer the time people spend in it (both these are true of bathrooms and toilets), the greater the effort you must put into the detail.

But as to the total effort and slog involved, smaller rooms mercifully mean it's done a lot quicker. I would have been completely fazed by having to undertake a shellwork scheme in a living room. Even a bathroom would have

RIGHT AND OPPOSITE: THIS LOO WAS A SAD AND NEGLECTED LITTLE ROOM UNTIL WE TOLD IT THAT IT COULD COME OUT AND PLAY. IT'S NOW ABSOLUTELY THE SMARTEST ROOM IN THE HOUSE, READY TO BE ENJOYED AT LENGTH.

meant a back-breaking amount of work. But in a room this size (generous for a loo), the task was manageable. Moreover, it meant that budgets could be kept to a reasonable level: in this case, the décor cost just £200.

When he saw the toile toilet finished, a friend of mine grumbled that if it were his, he would find it impossible to clean. But all the decoration is at the top of the room and less likely to gather dust. And my vacuum blows as well as sucks ...

The tented ceiling

I have only tented a ceiling once in my life: and that was for this book. And I can tell you that it is not particularly difficult, especially in a small room. However, finding a suitable fabric was more of a problem. I could have hunted the world over and not found a shell-motif paper or fabric that I like. So the alternative was to find one that suited the very eighteenth-century quality that the shellwork would have. The answer came in the form of a toile de Jouy which has a loose, charming design of peasants flirting in bucolic merriment. This would be just the job: light and joyful.

ABOVE AND BELOW: THE GHASTLY RECESSED SPOTLIGHT IN THE CEILING SUDDENLY FOUND A NEW IDENTITY AS THE VERY EPICENTRE OF THE ROOM'S DESIGN, CROWNED WITH A RING OF TRANSLUCENT SHELLS.

FIXING THE MATERIAL

YOU WILL NEED ...
12 mm x 12 mm timber
battening • plywood plate
30-38 cm (12-15 in) diameter
• Drill and drill bits • Screws
• Fabric • Scissors • Staple
gun with 12 mm (½ in) staples
• Sharp scissors

1 Drill and fix the battens to the top of the wall with screws. Get a good fix and do the same with the ceiling plate, screwing it into the exact centre of the ceiling.

2 Starting in one corner, cut material long enough to reach the centre, plus a little extra for working with. Staple to the batten every 7.5 cm (3 in), gathering lightly as you work.

3 As you work towards the middle of the wall, gather the fabric more often and more deeply. This balances the deep gathers that the fabric naturally creates at the room's corners.

4 Gather the fabric to the middle of the room, and gather your strength, too. Staple the fabric onto the plate, checking that the folds align with the dead centre. Staple in several places for security.

5 Trim excess fabric back to the innermost line of staples. You would normally disguise all this mess with a second ring or plate, covered with fabric.

I also needed a design that was made in matching paper (for the walls) and fabric (for the ceiling). It is surprising how few commercial ranges of paper and fabrics truly match, usually because they are printed in different factories using different inks and dyes. After embarking upon a search, we soon came upon just the thing and, even better, it was one of the cheapest of its kind on the market.

TIP

If the idea of all this tensioning and the expense of the fabric freak you out, consider doing this technique with muslin. You could even start with a bedhead corona.

The shellwork

Shellwork has a venerable history, forming part of Roman decoration and remaining popular throughout history, especially in the eighteenth and nineteenth centuries. It is now enjoying a revival among country house owners and although it can often be severely regimented, the style used here is altogether more naturalistic and grotto-esque. This actually makes it easier to do.

BELOW: THE WINDOW PELMET WAS MADE FROM A SHAPED PIECE OF PLY. THE SHELLS WERE GLUED TO IT WITH A GREATER SENSE OF DESIGN AND FLOW THAN ELSEWHERE IN THE ROOM.

FIXING THE PELMET AND SHELLS

1 I used a length of modern architrave for the base because it is straight, thin and angled. Paint it white as a background for the shells, cut, drill and fix it and then remove it to a flat bench.

2 Shellwork takes time, simply because you need to build the decoration, gluing shells on top of each other. A hot glue gun is indispensable. Don't cover the screw holes!

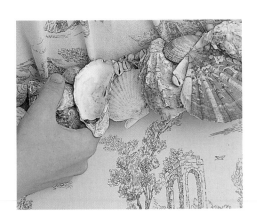

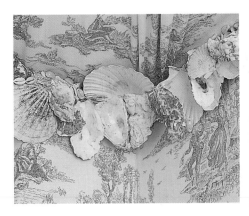

3 Once finished, the battens for each length of wall can be carefully lifted and screwed into place. Shells will, of course, fall off, but no matter – just stick them on again.

4 Repair any holes, add detail shells, and, most importantly, glue groups of large shells in the corners to hide the joints and provide a focal point. Finally, gather any strands of dried glue that tend to float around like spiders' webs.

YOU WILL NEED ... *Lengths of flat moulding • Shells of all shapes and sizes • Hot glue gun • A lot of patience*

TIP

I collect shells from the beach, but I also buy them in bulk from oyster farms, fishmongers and fish restaurants. I also use only plentiful native ones, not those shellfish that are culled in the Far East specifically for their shells.

Attention to Details

ABOVE: A GLASS PANEL WITH THE EDGES POLISHED WAS ORDERED FROM THE GLAZIER AS AN ALTERNATIVE TO TILES. ONCE INSTALLED WITH A TINY SILICONE BEAD AROUND THE EDGE, IT PROTECTS THE WALLPAPER FROM SPLASHES AND STAINS.

This room is even smaller than a bathroom, and consequently no wall is ever more than a matter of inches away from the eye. And because the loo is a room in which rumination and even concentration occur, any guest's eye will be inspecting the quality of finish and the menu of detail in this room, all in order to keep themselves occupied during their visit. Do not let them down, but put all your efforts in decorating this room to achieve the highest possible spec that you can.

WATER WORKS

In this case, we stripped the old copper water pipes in the room back to the metal and then polished them up to a decidedly Edwardian standard of mirror finish. Apart from anything else, doing things like this will afford you enormous pleasure, knowing that you've decorated at least one room in the house to the best possible standard.

One way of surprising people is to tread a slightly different route. Not a radical one that is often designed just to shock or deride, but a lateral route that will make them think, 'that's really clever'. The usual reason for doing this is because the professional decorator has spent the entire budget and so has to find a clever solution using materials to hand. Each example on these pages does just that and, not only are the ideas different, they are also good practical solutions to tricky problems. It has to be said that using materials in new ways is one of the most satisfying elements of interior design.

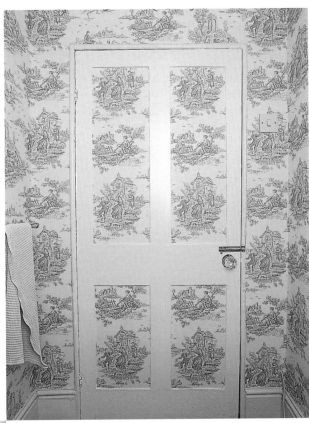

ABOVE: OFTEN DONE, BUT PARTICULARLY EFFECTIVE IN A TINY ROOM, THE DOOR PANELS WERE LINED WITH WALLPAPER, THE DOOR PAINTED TO MATCH THE PAPER BACKGROUND, AND AN ELEGANT CRYSTAL DOORKNOB FITTED.

ABOVE: IT WAS TOO EXPENSIVE TO BURY OR BOX-IN THE SINK WASTE PIPE, SO WE SOAKED FABRIC THAT MATCHED THE WALLPAPER IN DILUTE PVA GLUE AND WRAPPED THE PIPE INSTEAD. VERY EFFECTIVE!

TIP ▼

For a more traditional tented effect, look for striped fabric and matching wallpaper. Or for something a little lighter, use swathes of floating voile. The walls may need painting first, though, as voile is so translucent.

The *Essentials*

Transforming your bathroom into a palace of dreams is all very well, but you need to get the basics right. It is not enough for the room to look good, it must also provide enough space for human beings to move around and ablute in comfort. This section of the book guides you through the design process and gives you key information about choosing fittings, floorings, suitable surfaces and accessories.

Layout

The only other room that the bathroom compares to in terms of price is the kitchen. Both are expensive because the bones – plumbing, electricity, permanent fixtures – are so difficult to get right. And they can be a very expensive mistake if you get them wrong. It makes sense then to plan a bathroom in the same detail as you would a kitchen. You need graph paper on which to draw a scaled plan of the room; and you need cut-out templates of fixtures drawn to the same scale (most manufacturers provide accurate dimensions; many also provide the paper and templates – little outline drawings of their products in plan).

PLANNING

Before you start playing houses and moving the shapes around, however, you must mark on the other immovables in the room: windows and doors (remember you must be able to open the doors); cupboards, radiators and towel rails; and anything else you want to keep in its present position. You should also mark where the existing plumbing is, as this will give you some idea how expensive it will be to relocate it. Include the layout of existing water pipes, sewage ducts and ventilation ducts. There may be local water or building regulations that would make it almost impossible to move them.

If you are ecologically minded, you could also consider fitting bath and basin waste-water drains to an external pipe leading to a water butt. Most plants are happy to drink soapy water – particularly in drought conditions. Programming the water temperature correctly from the boiler will also save fuel and money. Baths really only need the addition of cold water if the temperature is set too high. A seven-day timer allows you to adjust water usage

ABOVE: CONSIDER CUSTOM-BUILDING A SHOWER UNIT TO FIT NEATLY IN AWKWARD SPACES.

LEFT: IF YOU ARE
LUCKY ENOUGH
TO HAVE A LARGE
SPACE, PLACE
THE BATH IN THE
MIDDLE OF THE
ROOM.
VERY ROMAN!

from day to day according to what you are doing during the week.

Now look at the room and think about the design possibilities – then with your graph paper and templates see whether they would work in practice. Make sure the basin allows enough space for washing and shaving in comfort. Check where the person using it will need to stand – they should have about 40 cm (20 in) space on each side and 70 cm (28 in) in front. This is especially important if you plan to site the basin in a corner. If you box in the basin, you must allow kick space at the bottom for feet – 10 cm (4 in) or so – and the basin must be at the front of the unit so as not to put too much stress on your back.

MAKING SPACE

A standard bath measures 1700 x 700 mm, but again you need to allow a 70 cm (28 in) wide space alongside the bath for getting in and out. You should also have 70 cm (28 in) clearance in front of the loo and bidet. Showers require a minimum of 80 cm (31 in) of space to step in and out. As you plot the position of fixtures, show these extra spaces as dotted lines around the room.

RIGHT: ALWAYS BEGIN WITH THE PLAN. THE LAYOUT OF THE ROOM IS CRUCIAL AND THERE MAY BE SEVERAL WAYS OF INCLUDING EVERYTHING. HOWEVER, ONE LAYOUT WILL WORK ESPECIALLY WELL.

You might well find that the existing layout was chosen for a purpose – or, conversely, why it has never worked very well. I devised all sorts of alternatives for the owners of the Portuguese Bathroom (see pages 38-49), only to conclude that the previous occupants had got it right, and that there was no other solution!

Don't be disheartened by how cramped your bathroom space appears. Catalogues give the impression that everyone else enjoys palatial bathrooms, but that's only because they are shot in enormous warehouse-style studios. You wouldn't really want a cavernous space; it could be difficult to heat and you would always find you needed something that is a walk away.

DESIGN WITH COMMON SENSE

Plans have one major flaw – they are horizontal only. You must also think about the height of each person in the household. Small children can crack their heads against the corner of a pedestal basin; tall men will tweak their backs bending low over one to wash. You might have to consider boxing-in for the former; putting it on a plinth for the latter. Perhaps there is a little nook you

could utilize for the bidet, but not if you hit your forehead on a beam every time you stand up. Similarly, shelving might be a great idea, but not where it is going to concuss someone getting out of the shower.

PUTTING IT INTO PRACTICE

Once you have decided where the key pieces – bath, basin, loo, bidet – are going, try to imagine yourself using them. Have you allowed enough knee and elbow room? Is the towel rail close enough to the bath? Where is the loo roll holder going to be positioned? Where are you going to keep children's bath toys, shaving gear, make-up and medicines? Could the door be rehung to open the other way, so opening up another few feet of space? Check, too, that the floor joists are strong enough to take the weight of your chosen bath. Cast iron roll-tops look wonderful, but you might have to strengthen the floor. If you are installing a shower for the first time, you need to think about how deep the drop is from the tank to the shower head. If it's not enough, the shower will only trickle unless boosted by a pump. Don't scrimp on plumbing for it – you may need to have it fed from both the hot and cold tanks, otherwise anyone using it will risk being scalded one moment and frozen the next.

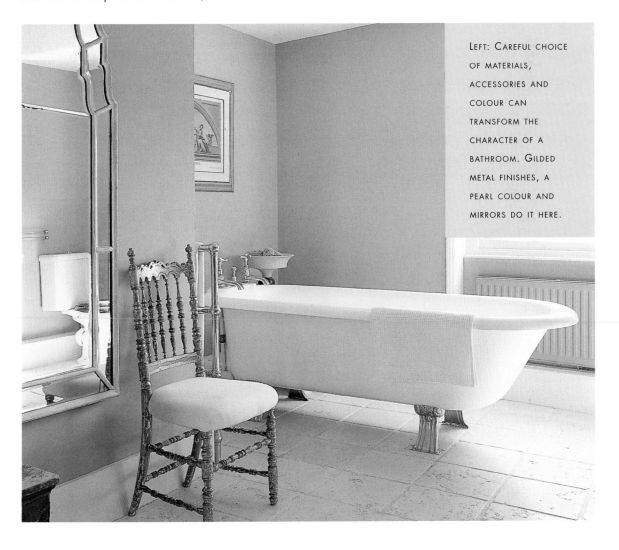

LEFT: CAREFUL CHOICE OF MATERIALS, ACCESSORIES AND COLOUR CAN TRANSFORM THE CHARACTER OF A BATHROOM. GILDED METAL FINISHES, A PEARL COLOUR AND MIRRORS DO IT HERE.

BUDGETING

While you are planning the layout, it is also worth taking a long, cool look at your budget. Fixtures may seem expensive, but they will only account for about half of the total cost. An awful lot of money will be swallowed up paying professionals to install everything safely for you. A plumber and electrician are essential – don't risk your own safety or that of your family attempting a DIY job here. You might also need to employ a carpenter to box in everything well; a builder for structural and plastering work; and a tiler – particularly if you are using hand-made tiles which are irregular in shape and colour. The decorating is the only task that you can probably undertake yourself. On top of all those wages, you will need to find the money for all those special extras: lighting, flooring, tiles, paint and fabric.

THE FINAL CHOICES

Don't expect your bath and basin to arrive looking as they do in the catalogue either. In fact, you will find that in addition you will have to order essentials such as plugs, waste traps, cistern handles and taps separately. It's well worth writing down all the items you need just to plumb in the bathroom. In the Portuguese Bathroom, for example (see pages 38-49), my list was something like the items listed below.

- Bath in white
- Mixer taps (spout not required).
- Chrome waste, plug, overflow, and chain to match

- Washbasin in white, two tap holes, no pedestal
- Chrome full taps to match
- Chrome waste, plug, overflow, and chain to match
- Back-to-wall WC
- Low-level cistern
- Porcelain and chrome WC handle
- Antique pine finish seat and lid with chrome hinges
- Pump unit
- Chrome shower mixer and head

ABOVE: A SUNKEN BATH MAY SOUND NAFF, BUT IT CAN WORK VERY WELL IF IT IS INCORPORATED INTO THE RIGHT SCHEME, AS HERE, AMONG MATCHING, LOW, SCULPTURAL FITTINGS.

LEFT: THE ARRANGEMENT OF BATHROOM 'FURNITURE' CREATES STRONG VISUAL IMPACTS. BATHS ARE BIG OBJECTS AND EASILY PROVIDE A FOCUS FOR THE ROOM.

Just writing it down in cold black-and-white tells you just how expensive it could end up being. But better to know now — and budget accordingly – than end up with a half-finished bathroom and a hefty overdraft.

Stand at the door of the bathroom and try to imagine where all the pipes will go – you don't want it to look like spaghetti junction, but it has to function properly. Hiring a good plumber will be a large chunk of your budget, so listen to the advice he or she gives: for example, 10 cm (4 in) diameter pipes, the ones used for waste from loos, take up a lot of room and can't cross joists under the floor. However, you could run them round the walls and box them out of sight, so creating a low-level shelf.

Another solution is to raise the bath onto a platform and conceal large pipes within this. But this is not a very practical idea if you have small children. Instead, perhaps you would do better to create a false wall behind the fixtures, so that plumbing can subsequently be hidden behind it. This has the advantage of creating valuable storage space (you can build cupboards or shelves into the niches you create) but it will reduce the dimensions of the room. Each solution has its advantages and disadvantages.

Baths

These are available in a number of different materials. Traditional cast iron is very durable, but also very heavy – in the worst instance you might need to reinforce your flooring. Cast iron helps your bath water stay warm, and also has some sound-insulating qualities. It also bonds well with the enamel finish, rendering the bath more scratch- and stain-resistant than if it were made from synthetic materials. However, because of the weight of cast iron, there are fewer shapes and sizes available than in acrylic or pressed steel ranges.

Pressed steel is the cheaper version of cast iron; it, too, has an enamelled finish. It is lighter, and comes in a good choice of colours and shapes, and there are now designs that are pressed with rolled edges to simulate cast iron. However, pressed steel doesn't have the insulating qualities of cast iron.

Acrylic used to have a bad name, but in fact there are some excellent upmarket acrylic designs on the market now. One of its advantages as a material is that it lends itself to precise and detailed styling – in other words, it can be moulded into all sorts of shapes. It is also light, and that means you can opt for a larger bath, an unwise choice in cast iron. However, make sure you buy reinforced acrylic as this gives a rigid, well-insulated finish.

Recently, manufacturers have begun to

BELOW: THE CLASSIC VICTORIAN ROLL-TOP IS STILL THE MOST PRACTICAL STYLE.

use stainless steel as a fourth option. Once it was only used in hospitals, but now influential designers such as Philippe Starck have turned their attention to its sleek, chic qualities, producing baths, and whole suites, that are unexpectedly attractive and comfortable.

STYLING DETAILS

Once you have selected the right material for your bathroom, you can turn your attention to colour and style. Corner baths are useful in awkwardly-shaped or small rooms, even if most of the available designs are hideous. Asymmetric baths also make use of irregular dimensions and give you a

BELOW: ACRYLIC BATHS CAN COME CONVENIENTLY MOULDED AND WITH HANDLES.

ABOVE: SHAPED ACRYLIC BATHS ARE
VERY USEFUL FOR FITTING INTO
AWKWARD CORNERS, ESPECIALLY IF
YOUR SPACE IS RESTRICTED.

wider place to sit than where your feet
go. These are a little more acceptable to
look at. Double-ended baths are a must if
you like to bathe with your partner – no
more arguments about who is sitting on
the plug-hole with their back to the taps.
They are also a great idea if you bathe
children together. Sunken baths look

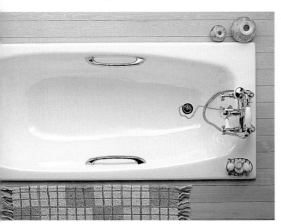

glamorous, in a kind of early 1970s way
(a style rapidly making a rather
unwelcome comeback), but you might
not think so when the time comes to
clean one. You will also need a structural
engineer to check that the floor can
support its weight. A chic alternative is

ABOVE: THE MARKET SUPPORTS MANY
DIFFERENT AND UNUSUALLY DESIGNED
PRODUCTS. BUT DO SIT ON AND IN THEM IN
THE SHOWROOM – THEY HAVE TO WORK!

to set the bath into a low platform,
surrounding it in the middle of the room
or up against one wall, with steps
forming at least one side.

With baths, the golden rule is, buy the
biggest you can. The average bath
measures 1700 mm long, but it makes
all the difference to be able to lie down
and stretch out comfortably in one that is
1800 mm long, or even larger. If you
really don't like bathing at all, and much
prefer to shower, then maybe a sit-down
tub with shower over would be a better
choice. These are smaller and deeper
than conventional baths, and are a good
choice for elderly or disabled people.

Showers

These are more economical than baths, and many people favour them for their speed and 'wake up' qualities. However, there is nothing exhilarating about turning one on and having water trickle down onto your neck – particularly if it veers from being an icy trickle one minute to a scalding one the next. The installation of a good pump is essential for most showers, but if you have a combination boiler you may not be able to fit one. You must have about a metre (yard) between the bottom of your water storage cold tank and the top of the shower head if you are not using a pump – the greater the distance (fall), the better the pressure.

Take advice from your plumber about whether you need a pump and, if you do, whether it needs to pump the whole bathroom (unlikely unless it's a bathroom in an attic) or just the shower. If your bathroom takes hot water from the tank and cold water direct from the mains, the pump may not be able to handle the difference in pressure between the two. In the Portuguese Bathroom on pages 38-49, a new cold feed had to be installed from the attic to the bathroom just to cope with this problem.

THE HEAD AND CONTROLS
Of course, no shower is half-way decent without a good shower head. These range from hand-held hose ones (very

ABOVE: GLASS CUBICLES MAY BE STYLISH, BUT THEY CAN MAKE YOU FEEL JUST ABOUT AS PRIVATE AS A GOLDFISH IN A BOWL.

good for washing hair in the bath and rinsing down animals), to those on slider bars, to types fixed to the ceiling or wall. They come in styles to suit every type of bathroom. Strategically placed body jets can massage your body in much the same way as a whirlpool bath does. Steam showers are also available.

RIGHT:
THE CHOICE
OF SHOWER
FITTINGS IS
INCREDIBLE.
MOST LOOK
LIKE PROPS
FROM *STAR
WARS*.

over the bath. If you have no choice but to combine the two, choose a bath that is as wide and flat-bottomed as possible.

Shower cubicles come in a range of styles and materials, some with accessories such as seats and towel rails, but they can be difficult to integrate well into an existing bathroom. Take a look at your plan and see whether there is a niche that could be utilized for a shower. For the Hedonist's Bathroom on pages 26-37, we went so far as to move a partition wall (between the bathroom and the landing) by 18 cm (7½ in) to provide enough space for a shower cubicle. Position the controls near the door so they can be pre-set before you get in, and make sure the shower walls, floor and ceiling are waterproofed and that the rest of the bathroom is also protected from splashes.

ABOVE: A TILED, PURPOSE-BUILT CUBICLE IS PERFECT AND PRIVATE. IF IT'S LARGE ENOUGH, YOU DON'T NEED A DOOR.

Shower controls also offer a bewildering choice, but the important thing is to have a thermostatic control to maintain the water temperature no matter what other appliances are being used in the house.

SHOWER CUBICLES
If you have the space, install a separate shower cubicle rather than having one

LEFT: A SIMPLE, HINGED GLASS SCREEN IS THE PERFECT SOLUTION FOR A BATH. MAKE SURE YOU CHOOSE A BATH WITH A LONG, FLAT BOTTOM.

Basins

Like the bath, the basin is another item that you should buy big. After all, you will probably use it for more than just splashing your face – rinsing out tights, washing hair, fighting over the toothpaste, and so on. Whether you conceal pipes behind a pedestal or a syphon cover is a matter of personal preference. Pedestals look elegant, but have the disadvantage of being at a fixed height. If you are tall and want a basin set higher than the standard, it would be better to do without the pedestal and set the basin into a cupboard top or unit (known prissily as a vanity unit) to whatever height is comfortable. Boxing-in unsightly pipes is

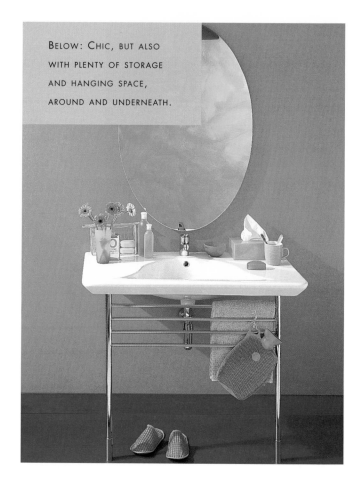

BELOW: CHIC, BUT ALSO WITH PLENTY OF STORAGE AND HANGING SPACE, AROUND AND UNDERNEATH.

LEFT: THIS BASIN LOOKS BEAUTIFUL, BUT WHERE ARE YOU SUPPOSED TO PUT ALL THE ODDS AND ENDS?

made easier with a vanity unit. Make sure that wall-mounted designs are securely fixed to a load-bearing wall.

TAP HOLES

Check that any tap holes are in the position you want. As with baths (see page 39), it might be better to buy a basin without holes, and drill them on site. When positioning the basin,

LEFT: VERY SMALL
CLOAKROOM
BASINS MUST BE
DEEP ENOUGH TO
AVOID SPLASHING.

ABOVE: THIS EXTRA-DEEP BASIN LOOKS GREAT
BUT UNLESS YOU ARE PLANNING ON WASHING
A LOT OF CLOTHES BY HAND IT IS NOT OVERLY
PRACTICAL FOR A BATHROOM.

consider how high the taps will be – you
don't want to continually bang yourself
on the forehead as you lean over to rinse
out your mouth.

BASIN DESIGN

Be careful about contemporary, minimal
designs. The Golden Age of sanitary
ware design was the late 1900s and
items from then have plenty of ergonomic
lessons to teach us. A good basin should
have areas to the side for siting the soap
and tooth mugs, and they should drain
freely into the bowl. Taps should be sited
well back and the front lip should be as
narrow as possible to prevent you from
straining your back when leaning over.

ABOVE: CORNER BASINS ARE IDEAL FOR
SQUEEZING INTO CRAMPED SPACES SUCH AS A
DOWNSTAIRS LOO OR SMALL SPARE BEDROOM.

Toilets and Bidets

Most people don't seem to worry about trying out beds in showrooms, but have an aversion to sitting on the loo in one. This seems a shame as you do want to buy a design that is comfortable. There are lots of styles and colours available, but the main choice comes down to whether you are going to opt for an old-fashioned high-level cistern or the more conventional low-level one. Both have a cistern and pan separated by a flush pipe. Make sure your plumber fits it correctly: there is a minimum height below which it may not flush correctly. The more modern, close-coupled loo has a cistern which is attached to the pan (this is the type we fitted in the Toile Toilet on pages 50-7), but you will have to ensure that you allow extra space for operating the flush lever.

BOXING IT IN

Discretion is assured with the back-to-wall pan: the cistern is concealed behind a false wall or duct, and the pan can even be wall-hung (so, in this case, check the wall can support the weight). The pan in the Portuguese Bathroom (see page 39) is a floor-mounted, back-to-wall type where not only the cistern but also half the pan have been carefully tiled in to a two-tier box structure. What a throne – a creative solution to lying in the bath and having to gaze at a boring old water closet!

On the subject of loo seats, I wonder if I am the only person to have an aversion to tricksy painted ones? I know it's witty to gild or marble the seat but I can't help feeling that the humour is, well, a little lavatorial? Wooden loo seats are doubtless more upmarket than plastic ones, but unless you check carefully, they are more likely to have been made out of some composite material such as MDF with a veneered wooden seat. I go for

ABOVE: VERY FEW TOILET DESIGNS ARE TRULY DELIGHTFUL. BOX, OR HALF-BOX, THEM IN, AND YOU WILL TIE THEM INTO THE ROOM'S OVERALL DESIGN A LITTLE MORE.

solid English oak, a mighty timber to
support a bottom.

BIDETS

There seems to be a reluctance to use
bidets properly, but they are great for all
kinds of uses; washing feet, soaking
underwear, and cleaning up semi-house-
trained toddlers. If you have the space,
fit one. Choose between floor-standing
or wall-mounted; tap-filled or supplied
from under the brim. Make sure it is
plumbed in correctly, and positioned so
there is plenty of room for your legs.

ABOVE:
CONTEMPORARY
FITTINGS CAN,
FROM A VERY
FEW SUPPLIERS,
BE VERY CHIC.

BELOW: IN A MULTI-PURPOSE
BATHROOM, TRY TO PLACE THE
LOO IN A CORNER. IT HIDES
IT A LITTLE AND ALSO
PROVIDES A SENSE OF
SECURITY WHEN SAT UPON.

ABOVE: IF YOU'RE TALL LIKE
ME, BUILD YOUR TOILET
PAN ON A PLINTH FORMED
FROM CEMENT OR TILES
TO GET SOME EXTRA
HEIGHT. IT'S MUCH MORE
COMFORTABLE TO SIT ON!

Taps

Put some time aside just to choose the taps. If you don't want them spoiling the lines of the bath or basin, buy them wall-mounted, but bear in mind the hassle this will cause the plumber and tiler. If you don't want the boredom of turning them on or off, you can buy all sorts of lever or push operated designs.

TAPPING THE STYLES

There are tall taps, low taps, retrospective taps and forward-thinking taps. There are taps that come cheap and taps that break the bank. But by the time you find the ones you want, you really won't care. The taps fitted in the Portuguese Bathroom shown on page 43 came with the basin on which they are fixed. In this room, nothing matches,

ABOVE: THE TRADITIONAL ARRANGEMENT OF SHOWER AND MIXER IS IDEAL FOR A FAMILY BATHROOM. THERE IS LESS DANGER OF SCALDING FROM A SINGLE HOT TAP AND IT IS VERY PRACTICAL.

LEFT: CONVENTIONAL TAPS SHOULD BE CLEARLY MARKED HOT AND COLD AND SHOULD PROJECT AS LITTLE AS POSSIBLE OVER THE BASIN EDGE.

and in a room such as this where the proportions are reasonable and the decoration and furniture design strong, it doesn't matter.

Do bear in mind that there are many charlatan taps out there, cheap versions that seem to be well-made. Test them in the showroom for weight (heavy means good), wobbly handles and plastic 'enamel' caps that scratch easily.

RIGHT: A STYLISH ARRANGEMENT IS TO HIDE MUCH OF THE PLUMBING IN THE WALL. REDOLENT OF EDWARDIAN SET-UPS, WE DID IT IN THE PORTUGUESE BATHROOM ON PAGE 39.

LEFT: A MIXER SET IS EXCELLENT BECAUSE IT CAN PREVENT SCALDING FROM A HOT TAP, BUT THE ARM MUST SWIVEL AWAY FROM OVER THE BASIN.

Storage and Accessories

If you think you're all spent up by now, you are sadly mistaken: bathrooms need other pieces of furniture, too. Don't underestimate your storage needs. You will need a home for everything from loo rolls and bath toys to cleansing supplies and shaving gear. Add to that the dirty linen, muscle-toning weights, medicines, baby bath, clean towels, bulk-bought nappies, and you begin to see the problem. In fact, the best thing to do is write a list of everything you need to house in the bathroom.

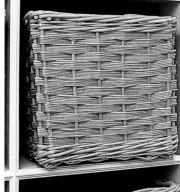

LEFT: MODULAR STORAGE UNITS LIKE THESE ARE USEFUL AS THEY CAN ADAPT TO CHANGES OF USE.

ABOVE: A LUXURIOUS SOLUTION IS TO BUILD FITTED STORAGE, ESPECIALLY IF THE ROOM DOUBLES AS A DRESSING ROOM.

BELOW: HANGING UNITS ARE A NOVEL VARIATION ON TRADITIONAL 1920s CHROME FIXTURES.

ABOVE: DON'T SPEND MONEY ON TAPS; INSTEAD, INVEST IN GOOD MATCHING ACCESSORIES.

STORAGE STYLE

The next decision is whether to incorporate built-in storage space into your design, or invest in custom-made pieces such as melamine cabinets or plastic-coated racks. If you can't fit in the former and hate the look of the latter, don't despair – you can achieve a lot with open shelving, different-sized wicker baskets and a tarted-up chest-of-drawers or cupboard. In other words, save your money for the accessories. Towel rails, soap dishes, toothbrush holders, loo roll holders, bathroom mugs, waste bins, bath mats and towels are those essential finishing touches – the ones between you and your bank manager.

RIGHT: TOWEL RAILS CAN BE HEATED, EITHER ELECTRICALLY, OR VIA THE CENTRAL HEATING.

ABOVE: CONTEMPORARY FITTINGS ARE RISKY. UNLESS VERY PLAIN, THEY CAN SOON LOOK DATED.

Lighting

Consider this: a bathroom has to function on two levels – a practical place in which to wash; and an inviting room in which to retreat. The two are not necessarily at odds with each other, but every design decision must recognize both roles. Lighting is no exception.

In other words, it is flexibility that counts. But to design a truly flexible lighting scheme means thinking ahead: wires have to be positioned in the right place before tiles are slapped on the walls and flooring glued to the boards. Quite rightly, there are very strict rules governing the installation of bathroom lighting, which means taking advice from a reputable electrician before writing out a huge cheque for fittings. If fittings are likely to get wet (and there is a European definition of what this means, which is surprisingly stringent), they must be completely enclosed to avoid possible shorting and electrical shocks. A pull-cord switch is the only safe option inside the bathroom, but you can have other switches – such as dimmer ones – wired outside the door.

MOOD PLANNING

When assessing your bathroom's lighting needs, first take a look at how much natural light you have. Remember it is a room that is used mainly in the morning and the evening, so it's not a lot of help if it is flooded in glorious sunshine at

midday. Think, too, of how the light changes through the seasons – not just in amount, but in quality. This should give you some indication of how much artificial light is needed in order to boost the natural.

When planning your lighting, you need to take account of the quality of light needed in specific places within the bathroom; the type of fitting that would achieve it, and the style that would best suit the look of the bathroom. Plan as many light sources as you can, and make sure they do not all work from one switch. You need the option of choosing different fittings for different moods. A lighting trough or false ceiling means you can conceal wires and fittings without disturbing plasterwork.

ABOVE: A COMBINATION OF GLOWING SOURCES AND LOW-VOLTAGE CEILING-MOUNTED SPOTS, ARE IDEAL IN BATHROOMS.

LIGHTING TYPES

Convention allows for lighting to be divided into three principal areas in bathrooms: ambient, or general light, task lighting, and atmospheric lighting (such as a twinkling wall light or candles), discussed on pages 80-1.

Ambient lighting is overall lighting that should be relaxing, have no glare, and be without hard shadows – the opposite of the solitary bulb hanging from a central wire. More radiance is created if you replace it by piercing the ceiling with a scattering of low-voltage spotlights or just recessed mains voltage downlighters that can be used to wash a

ABOVE: CANDLELIGHT IS ESSENTIAL FOR BATHING. THE MIRROR HERE DOUBLES THE INTENSITY OF THE LIGHT PRODUCED BY THE ATTACHED SCONCES.

ABOVE: SOFT LIGHTING IS A MUST AROUND MIRRORS TO APPLY MAKE-UP AND TO SHAVE BY. ALWAYS CHOOSE LIGHTS DESIGNED FOR BATHROOMS.

wall with light. In a small bathroom, you could replace a bare bulb with a frosted glass fitting such as the one I used in the Canopied Bathroom (see page 18) to provide a source of light that has less glare and produces softer shadows. The Hedonist's Bathroom uses a combination of low-voltage ceiling lights with large, glowing spheres (see pages 32-3), both circuits being dimmable to create differing atmospheres, from purely bright and functional to quiet to slightly weird!

Task lighting concentrates lighting on one place to illuminate what you are doing more brightly. The trick is to shield the light source from your eyes to avoid glare and spots before the eyes. For example, you may want to position a light above the basin so that it makes shaving, eyebrow plucking or leg waxing easier. You could mount it in a recess in the ceiling, or behind a pelmet as I did in the Portuguese Bathroom (see page 49). Or you could invest in softly glowing lighting panels to position around the mirror (see the Hedonist's Bathroom, page 32). Although they produce direct light, these panels contain several light sources, which are

ABOVE: A FEW COMPANIES PRODUCE STYLISH LIGHTING FOR BATHROOMS. THIS PIECE COMES FROM A WELL-KNOWN OUTFIT – McCLOUD & CO.

individually very dim and create no glare to distract the eye.

CHOOSING BULBS

Spare a thought about the type of bulb you prefer to use. Tungsten ones give a warm light, which enhance colours and create a soft, relaxing glow. The best way to use these bulbs is to buy the highest wattage suitable for the chosen fitting and control intensity with a dimmer switch. Halogen bulbs are, in fact, a mix of tungsten and halogen. They work well in uplighters where the light is directed to the ceiling and then reflected back into the room.

Low-voltage halogen bulbs are smaller than most bulbs and give out a crisp, concentrated light. The intensity varies according to the fitting used. They are excellent for all types of accent and task lighting, and also for ambient lighting when many of them are used together. Existing light fittings designed for standard voltage bulbs can sometimes be converted for use with low-voltage ones through a transformer.

Fluorescent bulbs are tubes that come in a variety of lengths and colours. Unfortunately, names such as 'warm white' cannot be trusted – all too often they create a hard, glaring light that flattens a room and everything in it. If you are hard up and have no choice but to keep your existing fluorescent fitting, you could investigate filters, which look like slatted panels and disperse the light so that it is not so unforgiving. Circular or curved fluorescent tubes are more flexible as they can be adapted for different fittings, including designs in paper, glass and steel. However, fluorescent bulbs cannot be used with dimmer switches.

DOWNLIGHTERS

Light fittings, too, come in myriad styles, shapes and sizes. The ones most suitable for the bathroom ceiling are downlighters. These cast pools of light on the surface immediately below. They can be surface-mounted or recessed into the ceiling. Downlighters can be

LEFT: BATHROOM FITTINGS MUST COMPLY WITH REGULATIONS. LIGHTING SHOPS AND GOOD SPECIALIST BATHROOM SUPPLIERS WILL BE ABLE TO ADVISE.

ABOVE: ALTHOUGH I WOULD NOT SPECIFY LOW-VOLTAGE SYSTEMS THROUGHOUT A HOUSE, THEY COME INTO THEIR OWN IN BATHROOMS.

RIGHT: THE
TRADITIONAL
THEATRICAL MAKE-UP
LIGHTS WORK IN
BATHROOM FITTINGS
BECAUSE EACH BULB
IS LOW-WATTAGE
AND SO GLOWS
WITHOUT GLARE.

positioned to cast a wide or narrow beam, dull or bright, general or directional. Whether you want a wall bathed in light or a slim beam picking up the contours of a shell, they provide the answer.

Although I am not a wholesale fan of low-voltage halogen downlighters (they were invented for use in shops, not homes), I do believe they work to best advantage in two rooms in the house, the kitchen and the bathroom; especially the latter because of the way their light makes bathroom surfaces – ceramic, porcelain and polished metal – shine and twinkle in a very alluring way. Their

versatility is a godsend, but if you prefer something more period in style, wall-mounted fittings with glass shades also provide glare-free light (remembering always to use a fitting marked as being approved for use in bathrooms). If you have no choice but to make use of that one ceiling light, think about fitting a track of low-voltage spotlights. These will provide some directional lighting.

ATMOSPHERIC LIGHTING

Once you are happy with the functional lighting you have planned – a combination of general and task – it is time to consider atmosphere. This can be achieved both with special decorative lighting, and the ingenious positioning of mirrors, glass and water. Candles are the cheapest way to transform a room. Use as many as you can find – tall ones, dumpy ones, floating ones, church ones – then switch off the artificial lighting and pray hard for a shaft of moonlight to slice through the window. Nothing could be more romantic if you are sharing your bath. Mirrors, glass and other shiny surfaces also accentuate their effect.

If your present bathroom is rather grotty – and likely to stay that way for a while – remember that imaginative lighting can be one of the most inexpensive ways of reviving it. For instance, coloured glass bottles are all

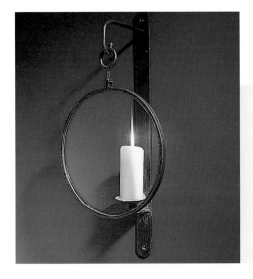

LEFT: TRANSLUCENT SHELLS, MIRRORS, GLASS, LENSES: ALL HAVE THEIR PLACE IN THE BATHROOM TO MODULATE THE LIGHT AND ALSO TO DELIGHT THE EYE.

the rage right now and a collection of these lit dramatically will give an edge to a room. Double the impact by positioning a mirror behind them. Quadruple it by hanging the shelf on which they stand near to the bath so that you can enjoy their reflections in the water. This will give the room an instant lift, adding a magical touch to a mundane space.

These tricks are cheap to pull off and they work very well in dimmed light, which is perhaps the biggest key to getting lighting right in your bathroom. Even if you do nothing else, and just leave a bare bulb hanging there, do get your bathroom re-wired so that the switch is outside the bathroom door, and then replace it for a few pounds with a dimmer. In this way, even a humble lightbulb on a flex will provide you with flexible lighting. It will also be one that you can supplement with a few candles now and then for a romantic glow.

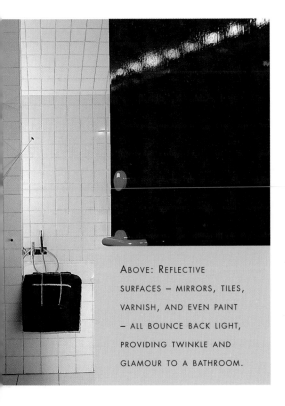

ABOVE: REFLECTIVE SURFACES – MIRRORS, TILES, VARNISH, AND EVEN PAINT – ALL BOUNCE BACK LIGHT, PROVIDING TWINKLE AND GLAMOUR TO A BATHROOM.

Flooring

The type of flooring you eventually choose should be determined by what you do in the bathroom; who uses it; how wet it is likely to get; the architectural character of the room; the colour scheme; how long you want the flooring to last; how much maintenance it will require; how comfortable you want it to be; how easy it is to lay; whether it must provide access to under-floor areas where pipes are laid, and last, but not least, budget. It's a tall order by anyone's standard.

MAKING YOUR CHOICE

A bathroom floor must fulfil certain requirements. It must be waterproof, non-slip and easy to clean. You will also like it more if it is kind to bare feet, can withstand wear and tear and looks great. Hard floors are the obvious choice – stone or ceramic tiles – but because of their coldness, they benefit from underfloor heating which is expensive to install. Avoid marble unless you are prepared to set up a long-term relationship with an osteopath.

At the other end of the spectrum are foam-backed carpets specifically designed with bathrooms in mind. Next to them lie the ever-enlarging ranges of natural floorings: seagrass, coir, hemp and jute. Of these, seagrass is reasonably waterproof, tough, firm but bearable underfoot (I used it in the Portuguese Bathroom, see page 39), coir and hemp are tough but quite unbearable to walk on, and jute is the softest (feeling almost like wool) but equally, since it is usually plain and pale, it wears poorly and shows stains all too easily. I know this all from experience.

HARD FLOORINGS

Hard ceramic or terracotta floors are usually the most expensive choice, but they are worth the extra money if you are planning on staying in your home for a long time.

ABOVE: MOSAIC TILES ARE VERY CHARMING AND COME FROM SOME MANUFACTURERS READY-FORMED INTO TILES.

Ceramic is still the most popular finish – not surprising when you consider just how many styles, textures and colours it comes in. You might opt for French Provençal, charmingly irregular handmade designs, glossy Italian colours, or more subtle rustic ones. For something a little more elaborate, opt for a mosaiced flooring. Any of these tiles can be laid onto a floor of waterproof blockboard or marine-grade plywood that will not warp. However, ceramic is not always the best choice if you have children: not only will toothbrush mugs and other fragile items smash to smithereens if dropped – but you run the risk of the tiles chipping under the impact. They are also noisy and cold, and unkind if you slip and fall. But then the same is true of any hard floor.

Quarry tiles are usually slightly softer and cheaper than ceramic ones – although just as durable; the ones in the Toile Toilet on page 51 were laid in the eighteenth century.

Slate has a beautiful, rippled surface making it more slip-resistant than many hard floors; it comes in a surprisingly varied range of greys, but they are perhaps now over-fashionable. York stone, granite and limestone all look handsome in the right setting, although I would not welcome them in my bathroom.

Brick, too, has become popular in recent years and can boast many ideal bathroom qualities – non-slip, waterproof, stain-resistant and warmer than ceramic tiles. However, it is really only suitable for ground floors because of its thickness. Even pebbled and cobbled floors have made an appearance in the style-setting bathrooms of glossy magazines. But good luck to them – they make a dirty, noisy, toe-stubbing surface. Only terrazzo compares to ceramic: this is a smooth, tough flooring made of marble chips set in concrete and ground smooth. It is thin enough to be made into tiles, sufficiently strong to withstand wear and tear, and has many colour and design options.

Among the hard floorings, wood might seem the last choice for the bathroom because of its antipathy to water but if you can overcome that problem through careful preparation and sealing, then you are on to a winner. Its advantages are warmth, durability, easy maintenance and beauty. But extremes of temperature, combined with frequent wetting, will cause it to shrink or swell. Also, don't attempt to lay a new wooden floor yourself unless you have checked and double-checked the position of water pipes underneath.

SEMI-HARD FLOORINGS

These floors can only be considered if they are waterproof and durable. On the whole, hardboard and chipboard – even if painted and varnished – are to be avoided, but if you are prepared to apply at least five coats of varnish and regularly touch up the paintwork, you can at least create your own fantasy floor very cheaply. Cork, on the other hand, is wonderfully versatile: lightweight but resilient; comfortable but durable; quiet but warm. Check, though, that you buy flooring-grade cork, and that it is laid and sealed properly. Underfloor heating will make it lift.

Vinyl is the mainstay of bathroom floors. It offers an incomparable number of patterns, textures, colours and thicknesses, both in tiles or by the metre. Add to that the fact that it is waterproof, stain-resistant, quiet, warm, and often inexpensive, and it is not difficult to see why it remains so popular. A more up-

market version is linoleum. This has shaken off its down-market reputation and been relaunched as a strong, flexible flooring that can be cut and laid in brilliant designs. However, any water caught underneath will cause it to rise.

Rubber flooring, as used in the Hedonist's Bathroom on page 36, has also taken its place as a tough, warm, safe and sophisticated choice. It offers

BELOW: COLOURWASHED WOOD REMAINS A FIRM FAVOURITE FOR FLOORING, EVEN THOUGH IT IS NOT ALWAYS THE MOST PRACTICAL CHOICE.

some bold colour choices and is much favoured by architects and designers who have moved it out of public utility settings and into domestic ones.

SOFT FLOORINGS

Soft floors really come down to different types of carpet. Those recommended for bathrooms often come in the nastiest shades and mixes imaginable, so it's worth looking at slightly more expensive, general-use carpet and checking whether it can be used in the bathroom. If you are buying a foam-backed one, check that the foam is of good quality. Rub it with your thumb fairly hard and if it flakes, don't buy it. Foam should be laid over paper or hardboard to stop it sticking to the floor, and I would be sceptical about using a foam-backed product if a lot of water is going to get spilt, since the foam will degrade when wet for prolonged periods. Don't lay shag pile in the bathroom – it might be soft and comfortable, but it will trap dirt and moisture and become easily matted. A top-quality woollen carpet is nearly always a safe choice.

CLASSIC COMBINATIONS

The final option is to introduce both hard and soft floors into the bathroom – perhaps a ceramic floor with strategically placed rugs for comfort underfoot. For safety's sake, make sure that rugs have mesh backing or nylon bonding strips to stop them slipping.

Whatever you decide to go for, don't budget tightly on the fitting. Floors are

BELOW: LINOLEUM, RUBBER AND ACRYLIC FLOORING CAN ALL BE CUT AND INLAID WITH INCREDIBLE PRECISION

expensive, and you want them to last. That means making sure the surface is properly prepared, that the right adhesives are used, that the cutting is confident and the edges are clean. They must not allow any water to seep through, and they must be absolutely even for safety. On a decorative level, even the plainest of floors will dominate a room purely because of its size. Don't be too influenced by fashion because of this: simplicity is often best.

Walls

Once you have solved all the functional problems of your new bathroom, you can get on and enjoy yourself, and start decorating. Lighting and flooring may play their parts, but there is no doubt that the quickest and easiest way to transform any room is with the walls. In most rooms, of course, this can be done with a gallon of paint; in the bathroom, it can work out rather more expensive.

The biggest challenges for bathroom walls are withstanding the combination

LEFT: MACHINE-MADE MOSAICS ARE EASY TO APPLY AND COME GLUED ONTO LARGE SHEETS. HOWEVER, THEY CAN LACK CHARACTER.

of moisture and heat that results in condensation, plus the task of resisting the daily rigour of being sprayed with hot water and scoured by children's soapy hands. Ceramic tiles have always been the most popular choice for the job because they are so tough. They are also (sometimes) attractive, durable and infinitely varied in their patterns. You can choose between sheets of small mosaic ones, glittering glass tiles, textured hand-made designs and a staggering array of truly brilliant colours. And if you want to change your existing tiles, don't waste your time prising the old ones off the wall. Tile manufacturers themselves recognize that the best surface to tile on is, er, tile ... and with waterproof adhesives and grout, this is extremely easy to do.

ABOVE: HAND-MADE MOSAICS HAVE THEIR OWN WOBBLY CHARM BUT THEY REQUIRE CAREFUL LAYING AND CAN BE SHARP-EDGED, SO WEAR PROTECTIVE GLOVES.

But now the down-side. Tiles can be astronomically expensive to buy and expensive to install. They are also perhaps creatively limiting when compared to some of the sheet materials available, such as perspex, shatter-proof glass and plastic laminates.

ABOVE: LARGE TILES PROVIDE AN UNUSUAL ALTERNATIVE FOR THE WALLS – NOT REDOLENT OF TILING AT ALL, MORE LIKE MARBLE PANELS.

PERFECT PAINT

Paint, of course, represents an approach to decorating that we can all understand and, even better, use on a more modest budget. Whereas ten years ago I was writing how water-based paints should be avoided in a bathroom and how oil-based ones were essential, thinking, and products, have changed immeasurably in that time. Of course, some (mainly traditional) paints are hopeless in any kind of humid environment. Distemper and casein-type paints will last no longer than five minutes, and limewash, at best a good exterior paint, will not be happy in such combinations of heat and steam. Even bog standard emulsion does not like high levels of humidity, because its PVA binders soften under the effects of heat and never become fully waterproof.

However, don't give up hope of using a water-based product. Water-borne acrylic paints are now available that when fully dry in a few days set to a tough, waterproof surface. They are very pleasant to use, especially in such a confined space as a bathroom, and are the paints we used in all the makeovers in this book. However, there are a few places I would still not use them: near a shower, because there is always a risk that acrylic paint will soften under the effect of hot water, and on woodwork. Call me an old stickler, but traditional oil-type paints brush out so beautifully, without leaving a single brushmark (unlike acrylics) and do not raise the grain of unpainted wood in the way any water-based product will. Acrylics have their uses on bathroom walls, but give me a litre of eggshell or silk any day.

DECORATIVE EFFECTS

One of my favourite techniques, and one quite suitable in a bathroom, is colourwashing. Although the name derives from the way colour was once added to distemper or whitewash, this process gives an effect of old paint and plaster. Any surface will do, as long as it has been well primed and sealed, although lining paper coated with two

RIGHT: BATHROOMS MEAN COMPLICATED LUMPS OF SANITARY WARE BOLTED ONTO THE WALL. HOWEVER, BY FINISHING THE VANITY UNIT AS THE WALL, THIS OWNER HAS SIMPLIFIED THE DESIGN, BEAUTIFULLY.

ABOVE: FOR PAINT FINISHES TO
WORK, THEY MUST BE VERY CAREFULLY
APPLIED. PUTTING DARK OVER A
LIGHT GROUND, AS HERE, CAN LOOK
A LITTLE DIRTY.

down afterwards, it'll be positively oozing with condensation ...'

However, decorators and architects have been using textured techniques for thousands of years, and the modern equivalents of their gessos are easier to handle and tough when dry. You can even texture ordinary paint with talcum powder or other thickening agents. For those who favour a chic 1990s French look, plain cement-rendered walls are all the rage – the rougher, the better (the French like their concrete). Cement can

BELOW: PROVIDING YOU ARE PREPARED TO BE
PAINSTAKING, PAINT EFFECTS – HERE, STENCILLING
– CAN BE WONDERFUL IN A BATHROOM.

applications of paint is the best surface – not least because colourwashing picks up all the imperfections, bumps and humps of a surface, and charmingly emphasizes them. Too much emphasis and the wall just looks tatty. Too little movement in the paint and the effect is anaemic. The idea, as shown on pages 46 and 47, is to produce something freehand, imperfect and rather clouded – a million miles away from the flat, regulated finishes seen in show houses.

If there is a new 'techniques' fad on the horizon, then it must be the use of textured surfaces. Totally impractical in a bathroom, of course: 'Mind that gritty wall, Mother, and don't forget to towel it

even be mixed with waterproofing agents, doing away with the need for expensive tiles, and it can be finished smooth or left gritty. White cement coloured with ochre pigments or even yellow sand produces a wonderful honey-coloured finish.

If you are plastering concrete walls, let them dry for at least two weeks before painting or sealing. Buy EVA sealant (the waterproof sister of PVA) and apply it in a mix of one part sealant to three parts water. You will need two coats or more; let it sink into the walls. You can have a lot of fun with plaster and I explain how to use it decoratively in the Textured Bathroom on pages 30-1.

And then, there is a final plea for an unfashionable wallcovering. Wallpaper in the bathroom has suffered from a bad press but, in fact, it works extremely well. There are plenty of washable and spongeable papers on the market, and many of the designs look great when combined with other materials such as tiles, wood or paint.

My own bathroom has a charming wallpaper with a grey eighteenth-century design, printed with waterproof inks. It is protected over the basin by a glass panel (see page 56). With a suitably patterned paper, you could cut out individual motifs and use them for a découpage scheme, sticking them onto the wall with a waterproof adhesive, then sealing with two or three coats of matt acrylic varnish. But don't use acrylic varnish anywhere near hot running water – over the bath, for instance – as it may go soft. Neither would I advise using EVA, as it will look unpleasantly shiny.

Two other two materials to avoid for finishes in the bathroom are polyurethane varnish, because it often blemishes and blooms white when used near showers, basins or baths; and shellac, because it tends to flake off when damp.

LEFT: IF YOU DARE, GO THE WHOLE HOG AND INSTALL THE BATH IN YOUR BEDROOM. OR JUST WALLPAPER THE BATHROOM TO LOOK LIKE A BEDROOM. ADD CURTAINS AND YOU GET AN EMPIRE BOUDOIR.

Useful addresses

Accessories and storage

CP Hart
Newnham Terrace
Hercules Road
London SE1 7DR
Tel: 0171 902 1000

Habitat UK
The Heal's Building
196 Tottenham Court Road
London W1P 9LD
Tel: 0171 255 2545

Homebase
Beddington House
Railway Approach
Wallington
Surrey SM0 0HB
Tel: 0181 784 7200

IKEA
225 North Circular Road
London NW10 0JQ
Tel: 0181 208 5600

McCord Mail Order Catalogue
Tel: 0990 535 455

Wickes
Wickes House
120-138 Station Road
Harrow
Middlesex HA1 2QB
Tel: 0181 901 2000

Flooring

The Amtico Company Ltd
Kingfield Road
Coventry CV6 5PL
Tel: 01203 861 400

Crucial Trading Ltd
P.O. Box 11
Duke Place

Kidderminster DY10 2JR
Tel: 0171 730 0075

Dalsouple
P.O. Box 140
Bridgwater TA5 1HT
Tel: 01984 667 233

Fired Earth
Twyford Mill
Oxford Road
Adderbury
Oxfordshire OX17 3HP
Tel: 01295 812 088

Forbo-Nairn Ltd
P.O. Box 1
Kirkcaldy
Fife
Scotland KY1 2SB
Tel: 0345 023 166

Lighting

CP Hart
Address as above.

IKEA
Address as above.

McCloud & Co.
269 Wandsworth Bridge Road
London SW6 2TX
Tel: 0171 371 7151

Sanitaryware

Doulton Bathrooms
Lawton Road
Alsager
Stoke-on-Trent ST7 2DF
Tel: 01270 879 777

CP Hart
Address as above.

Ideal-Standard Ltd
The Bathroom Works
National Avenue
Kingston upon Hull HU5 4HS
Tel: 01482 346 461

Twyfords
Caradon Bathrooms Ltd
Lawton Road
Alsager
Stoke-on-Trent ST7 2DF
Tel: 01270 879 777

Showers

Caradon Mira Ltd
Cromwell Road
Cheltenham
Gloucestershire DL52 5EP
Tel: 01242 221 221

Nordic
Fairview Estate
Holland Road
Oxted
Surrey RH8 9BZ
Tel: 01883 716 111

Wall treatments

Baer & Ingram
273 Wandsworth Bridge Road
London SW6 2TX
Tel: 0171 736 6111

Criterion Tiles
Wandsworth Bridge Road
London SW6 2UF
Tel: 0171 736 9610

Fired Earth
Address as above.

Grahams Builders' Merchants
96 Leeds Road
Huddersfield HD1 4RH
Tel: 01484 537 366

Acknowledgements

My thanks to the following in help with this book: Helen Chislett for help fore and aft; Martin Butler for building work; Darren Noade and Russell Hobson for assisting with painting and shellwork; Emma Callery, Gabrielle, Lucy and Rona at Phoebus for their patience; Daisy Goodwin for her help and guidance; Kate and Paul Quarry, Helen McAleer and Matthew Lyons for letting us loose in their homes; my agent, Jane Turnbull for her steadfastness, and my wife for her support and inspiration.

SUPPLIERS CREDITS

The author would like to thank the following for supplying items as listed below.
Pages 14-25 Tiles from Criterion Tiles, as above; flooring from Amtico, as above; paint, shower, fixtures and fittings from Homebase, as above. Pages 26-37 All fixtures, fittings, furniture, sanitaryware and lighting from CP Hart, as above; flooring from Dalsouple, as above, or from First Floor, 174 Wandsworth Bridge Road, London SW6 2 UQ, tel: 0171 736 1123 or Millers Specialist Flooring, 177 Leith Walk, Edinburgh EH6 8NR, tel: 0131 554 2408; plaster from Grahams Builders' Merchants, as above; chrome towel rail from Heal's, 196 Tottenham Court Road, London W1P 9LD, tel: 0171 636 1666. Pages 38-49 Bath, toilet and basin from Twyfords, as above; flooring from Crucial Trading, as above; shower from Caradon Mira, as above; fixtures and fittings from Homebase, as above; tiles from Criterion, as above.. Pages 50-7 Fabric & wallpaper from Baer & Ingram, as above; toilet, sink chrome taps and bottle trap from Twyfords, as above.

PICTURE CREDITS

BBC Books would like to thank the following for providing photographs and for permission to reproduce copyright material. While every effort has been made to trace and acknowledge all copyright holders, we would like to apologize should there be any errors or omissions.

Page 7: Robert Harding Picture Library (RHPL) (Polly Wreford/Country Homes & Interiors); Page 8: Elizabeth Whiting & Assocs (EWA) (Di Lewis); Page 9: The Interior Archive (Simon Brown); Page 10: EWA (Rodney Hyett); Page 11: © BBC (Paul Bricknell); Page 59 (tl, tr & bl) C P Hart, (br) EWA (Michael Crockett); Page 60 RHPL (Fritz von der Schulenburg/Country Homes & Interiors); Page 61 C P Hart; Page 62 Ideal-Standard Ltd; Page 63 RHPL (Mark Luscombe-Whyte/Homes & Gardens); Page 64 Ideal-Standard Ltd; Page 65 RHPL (Polly Wreford/Country Homes & Interiors); Pages 66-7 (tl, cr & bl) & 68 C P Hart; Page 69 (tl) Nordic Saunas Ltd, (cl) RHPL (Dominic Blackmore/Ideal Home), (br) C P Hart; Page 70 (r) C P Hart, (bl) Ideal-Standard Ltd; Page 71 (tl) IKEA, (tc & br) C P Hart; Page 72 © BBC (Paul Bricknell); Page 73 (t) C P Hart, (bl) Ideal-Standard Ltd, (br) © BBC (Paul Bricknell); Pages 74-5 C P Hart; Page 76 (cr) EWA (Michael Crockett), (bl) IKEA; Page 77 (tl) McCord Design, (tr & bc) C P Hart, (br) IKEA; Page 78 Fired Earth; Page 79 (tr) RHPL (Trevor Richards/Homes & Gardens), (bl) The Interior Archive (Fritz von der Schulenburg); Page 80 McCloud & Co; Page 81 (r) Earl Carter/Belle/Arcaid, (l) C P Hart; Page 82 EWA (Michael Dunne); Page 83 (t) EWA (Andreas von Einsiedel), (b) Arcaid (Ken Kirkwood); Page 84 Fired Earth; Page 85 EWA (Rodney Hyett); Page 86 Colin Poole; Page 87 RHPL (David Giles/Homes & Ideas); Page 88 Simon Kenny/Belle/Arcaid; Page 89 RHPL (Brian Harrison/Homes & Gardens); Page 90 The Interior Archive (Fritz von der Schulenburg); Page 91 (t) IPC Magazines Ltd/RHPL, (br) RHPL (James Merrell/Homes & Gardens); Page 92 RHPL (Tim Goffe/Country Homes & Interiors).
All other photography by Paul Bricknell, George Taylor and John Heseltine © BBC

Index